BETTER HOMES AND GARDENS®

INCREDIBLY AWESOME
CRAFTS FOR KIDS

INCREDIBLY AWESOME CRAFTS FOR KIDS
Editor: Sara Jane Treinen
Associate Art Director: Linda Ford Vermie
Project Manager: Jennifer Speer Ramundt

Crafts Editor, Photography: Beverly Rivers
Graphic Designer: Mick Schnepf
Publishing Systems Text Processor: Paula Forest
Contributing Photographer: Perry Struse
Contributing Writer: Judith Veeder
Contributing Illustrator: Sue F. Cornelison

BETTER HOMES AND GARDENS® BOOKS
An Imprint of Meredith® Books
Vice President and Editorial Director: Elizabeth P. Rice
Editor, Crafts Department: Sara Jane Treinen
Art Director: Ernest Shelton
Managing Editor: David A. Kirchner
Prepress Production Manager: Randall Yontz
Art Production Director: John Berg

President, Book Group: Joseph J. Ward
Vice President, Retail Marketing: Jamie L. Martin
Vice President, Book Clubs: Richard L. Rundall

WE CARE!

The Crafts Department at Better Homes and Gardens® Books assembled this collection of
projects for your crafting pleasure. Our staff is committed to providing you with clear
and concise instructions so that you can complete each project. We guarantee your satisfaction
with this book for as long as you own it. We welcome your comments and suggestions.
Please address your correspondence to Better Homes and Gardens® Books Crafts Department,
1716 Locust Street, LS-352X, Des Moines, IA 50309-3023.

© Copyright 1992 by Meredith Corporation, Des Moines, Iowa.
All Rights Reserved. Printed in the United States of America.
First Edition. Printing Number and Year: 10 9 8 7   97 96 95
Library of Congress Catalog Card Number: 91-62192
ISBN: 0-696-01924-8 (hardcover)
ISBN: 0-696-01984-1 (trade paperback)

Gather all your craft supplies, follow our easy step-by-step instructions, add your own spark and imagination, and you can create some terrific projects. Use paint and paper, glitter and glue, socks and rocks, cork and clay, or felt and floss to make things for yourself or gifts for your family and friends. You can make puppets for fingers and those on a string, clocks that tell time, Halloween ghosts and masks, colorful Easter baskets, cards that pop up, and books or book covers. Or, dye a T-shirt, build a bank, paint an umbrella, craft holiday decorations, or mold earrings and bracelets. We hope you have loads of fun with this book!

CONTENTS

PAINTING FUN

PAPER MAGIC

4

SHAPE, SCULPT, AND BUILD

PLAYFUL PUPPETS

DAZZLING DOLLS

READY, SET, CRAFT

Here are some tips for getting ready to do the projects in this book. Plus, there's a list of project ideas to make for special occasions or for yourself throughout the year 166–167

PAINTING FUN

SHIRTS TO DYE FOR

Here's a great way to turn a white cotton T-shirt into a smashing success. Turn the page to find four more terrific tie-dye ideas.

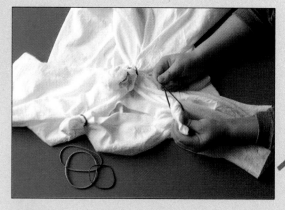

1 Cover your work area with the plastic drop cloth. Assemble all of the materials.

2 Place the T-shirt, front side up, on the table and smooth out any wrinkles with your hand.

3 To make the large circle on the body of the shirt, pull up the center of the shirt (front and back together) and gather the fabric. Twist a rubber band tightly at the bottom of the gathered bundle of fabric. Twist more rubber bands ½ to 1 inch apart coming up the fabric bundle.

TOOLBOX

- ▶ Plastic drop cloth
- ▶ 100% cotton T-shirt, prewashed and preshrunk
- ▶ Rubber bands
- ▶ Rubber gloves
- ▶ Fuchsia (hot pink) dye or color of your choice
- ▶ Small bowl for mixing dye
- ▶ Long-handled wooden spoon
- ▶ Two large enamel pans

8

4 In the same way that you gathered the center of the shirt, gather and wrap each shoulder area with rubber bands. Wrap each bottom corner with rubber bands.

5 Put on rubber gloves. Following the directions on the dye package, mix the dye with the wooden spoon in the small bowl. Pour the dye mixture into a large enamel pan, add more water, and stir again. (**Caution: If you are using a hot-water dye, be sure to have adult help and supervision.**)

6 Dampen the shirt under a running faucet. Squeeze out extra water. Dip the shirt in the dye pan and stir for the amount of time listed on the package or until the shirt is the desired color. Keep in mind that the shirt will look darker when wet.

7 Squeeze out the excess dye and place the shirt in the empty pan. Carry the pan to the sink and rinse the shirt until the water is almost clear. Remove the rubber bands and rinse the shirt again. *Note: Check the package instructions to see if adding salt to the rinse water is necessary to make the dye permanent.* Hang the shirt to dry.

Cut up an old cotton sheet to practice the tying methods shown here. Then dye more shirts to jazz up your wardrobe and dazzle your friends.

TIPS ON COLORS

Our samples are dyed with only one color on white fabric. If you want to use more than one dye color, or use different colors of fabrics, remember that the colors will combine with each other to make new colors. For example, yellow and blue will make green. The color of the fabric used also will affect the results.

Experiment on small scraps of fabric first. When using light and dark dyes together in a project, always dye the light color first.

KNOTTING Bundle or fold your fabric into a long "rope." Tie overhand knots along the bundle of fabric. Dampen the fabric and place it in the pan with the dye.

GATHERING Cut a piece of heavy string or cording slightly longer than the length of the fabric. Roll the fabric around the cording. Tie the ends together, pulling the rolled fabric into a tight, gathered circle. Complete the knot. Dampen the fabric and place it in the pan with the dye.

WORKING WITH DYES

Special dyes for tie-dyeing can be purchased in arts and crafts supply stores. These dyes, such as Deka, result in brighter, nonfading colors.

Dyes will stain your skin. Wear old clothes, an apron, and rubber gloves. Cover your work surface with plastic.

Read dye packages carefully. Water temperature is important. Cold-water dyes can be used in cold or warm water. Multipurpose dyes can be used in both cold and hot water. For best results, choose 100-percent natural fabrics, such as cotton, linen, or silk. Always prewash a new fabric before you dye it.

Some dyes require salt, baking soda, or vinegar to make the dye permanent. Read the instructions with your dye package to determine the specific directions for the dye you choose to use.

CLAMPING Pleat your fabric accordion-style. Clamp it with spring-type plastic clothespins along both long edges of the fabric. Dampen the fabric and place it in the dye pan.

MARBLING Gather the fabric into a ball and tightly wrap cotton string over and over in all directions. Knot the string. Dampen, then place it in the dye. Clip the string and unwrap the fabric. If the color is weak in an area, crumple the fabric into a ball again with that area to the outside. Tie and re-dye the fabric.

MARBLEIZING MAGIC

Dip paper into liquid starch and floating paint to decorate paper that can be used to create these 3-D Christmas ornaments. Turn the page and you'll find more clever ideas for this colorful paper.

1 Use the plastic spoon to mix 2 tablespoons of red paint with 2 tablespoons of distilled water in a paper cup. Add more paint or water, if necessary, to make a creamy mixture. Pour enough starch into the baking pan to measure 1 to 1½ inches deep. Skim the surface with a paper towel to remove any air bubbles.

TOOLBOX

- ▶ Jars of red, blue, and green acrylic paints
- ▶ Water
- ▶ Plastic spoon
- ▶ Paper cups
- ▶ Liquid starch
- ▶ 9x13-inch baking pan
- ▶ Construction paper
- ▶ Comb or feather
- ▶ Paper towels
- ▶ Tracing paper
- ▶ ⅛-inch-wide ribbon for hangers
- ▶ Glue stick

2 Dribble several drops of the paint mixture onto the starch. If the paint sinks below the starch surface, add a little more distilled water to the paint. Use a comb or experiment with other tools, such as a feather or stick, to swirl designs onto the top of the mixture.

3 Lay a sheet of construction paper on the top of the mixture, letting the middle of the page touch first. Smooth the outside edges of the paper over the mixture.

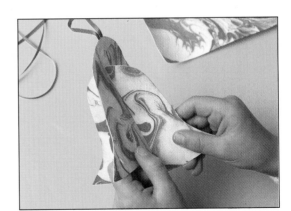

4 After about 15 seconds, lift the paper from the paint. Lay it, paint side up, on paper towels. Lay a paper towel on top of the paper. With the heel of your hand, press down on the paper towel to remove the excess paint. Pull off the paper towel. Repeat the pressing motion with another paper towel. Lay aside the marbled paper, paint side up, to dry.

Skim the surface of the paint mixture to remove the old paint. Repeat steps 2 and 3 to make another marbled sheet.

5 Use tracing paper and a pencil to trace the bell pattern on page 16. Cut out the pattern.

Rub the glue stick over the unpainted side of one sheet. Fasten the two marbled sheets together.

6 Trace two bell patterns on the marbled paper. Cut out the bells. On one bell only, cut a slit from the bottom of the bell up to the end of the blue line on the pattern. Cut one 4-inch piece of ribbon for the hanger. Gently pull apart the glued edges at the bell top and insert the ends of the ribbon. Press the edges back together.

7 Cut a slit from the top of the second bell up to the end of the red line on the pattern. Holding the bells perpendicular to each other, slip the bell with the hanger over the top of the second bell.

13

MORE MARBLEIZING PROJECTS

GIFT TAGS Cut a 3x5-inch rectangle from marbled paper and fold it in half. Cut a smaller rectangle from plain white paper and use a glue stick to fasten it to the inside of the tag. Punch a hole in the top left corner of the tag. Thread a folded 8-inch-long gold cord through the hole. Tie the ends to your package ribbon.

BOOKMARKS Glue a 2x7-inch poster-board rectangle to the wrong side of the marbled paper. Cut out the shape. Cover the shape with clear adhesive-backed vinyl. Thread a looped 12-inch-long piece of gold cord through a punched hole at the top of the bookmark. String beads onto the cording to add flair.

VALENTINE CARD

Fold a 5x8-inch sheet of marbled paper in half. Trace around the heart pattern on page 17. Place the pattern on top of the paper, matching the fold lines. Cut out the heart. Make a white paper lining for the card, using the heart card lining pattern. Glue the lining to the inside of the card. Make an envelope from marbled paper. (Take apart a small envelope and use it for your pattern.) Glue red foil to the inside back and flap of the envelope. Fold and glue the envelope, following the fold lines of the envelope you tore apart.

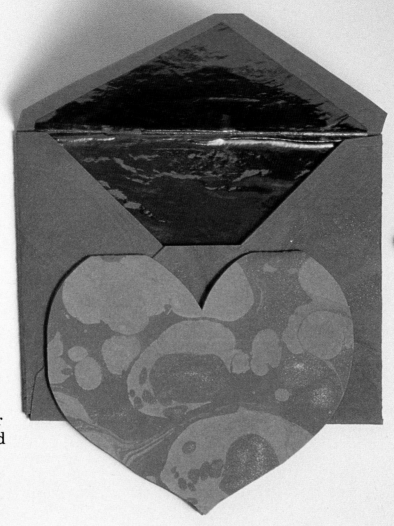

MAGNETS

Use the patterns on page 17 to cut shapes from marbled paper. Glue these shapes to cardboard. Cut out the designs. Cover the shapes with clear adhesive-backed vinyl. Cut strips of magnetic tape. Fasten a strip to the back of each shape.

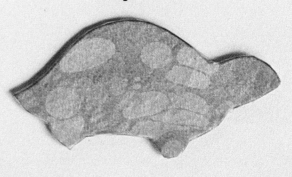

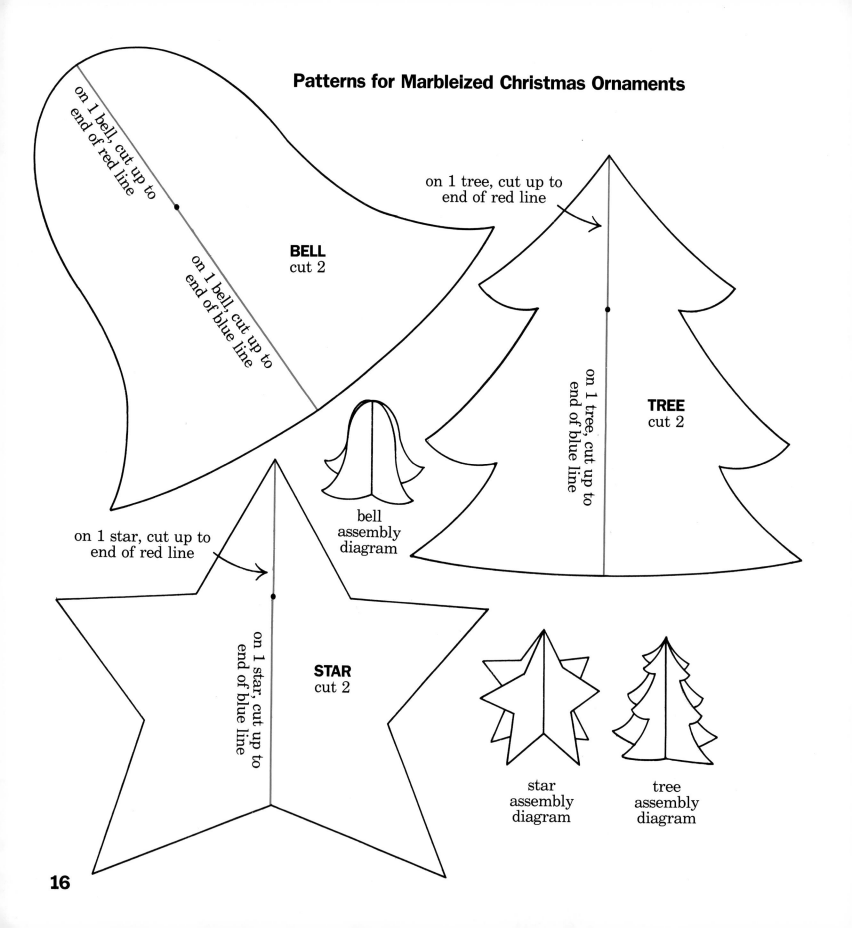

Patterns for Marbleized Christmas Ornaments

on 1 bell, cut up to
end of red line

on 1 bell, cut up to
end of blue line

BELL
cut 2

on 1 tree, cut up to
end of red line

on 1 tree, cut up to
end of blue line

TREE
cut 2

bell
assembly
diagram

on 1 star, cut up to
end of red line

on 1 star, cut up to
end of blue line

STAR
cut 2

star
assembly
diagram

tree
assembly
diagram

16

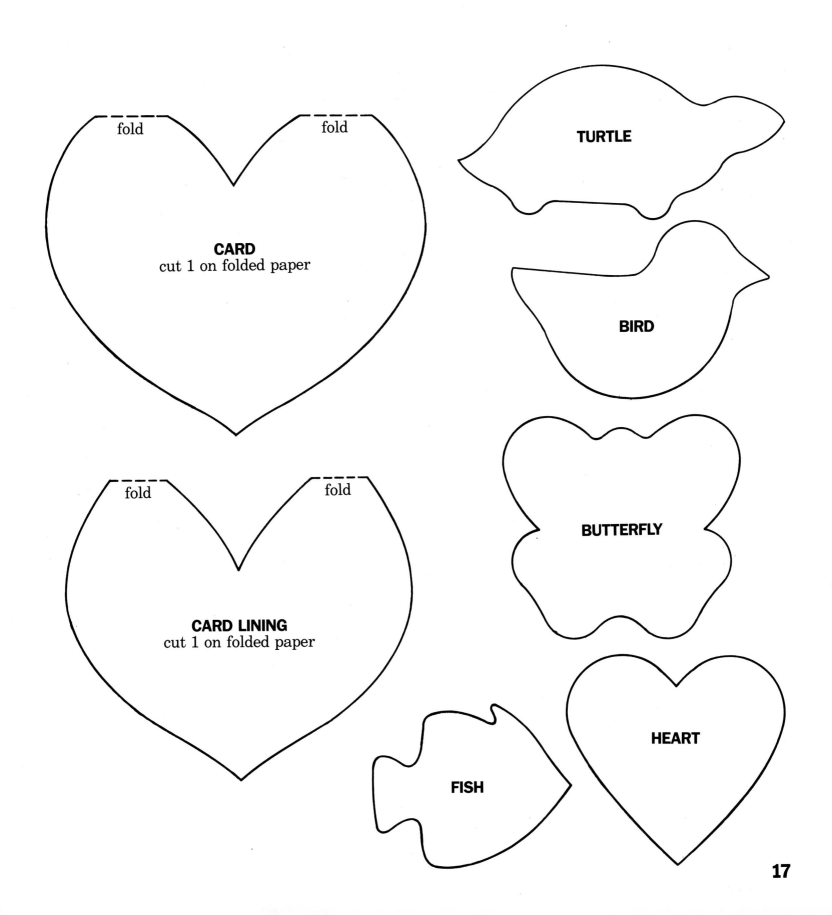

fold   fold

CARD
cut 1 on folded paper

fold   fold

CARD LINING
cut 1 on folded paper

TURTLE

BIRD

BUTTERFLY

FISH

HEART

17

fingerprints

You'll have a fun time using your fingers and paint to print the colorful gift paper shown here. See also the footprint design on the next page.

See also the footprint design on the next page.

TOOLBOX

- ▶ Large sheet of white paper
- ▶ Plastic plates
- ▶ Jars of acrylic paints in assorted colors
- ▶ Fine-tipped black felt pen
- ▶ Metallic stars

1 For the baby gift wrap, place a large sheet of white paper on your worktable. Pour some pink paint onto a plastic plate. Use your middle or index finger to paint six fingerprints on the paper for the head, body, arms and legs. Make more baby prints all over the paper. Let the paint dry completely.

2 Use the fine-tipped black felt pen to draw eyes, noses, mouths, and hair. The babies *below* show you several facial expressions you might draw.

1 For the Christmas tree gift wrap, place white paper on your worktable. Pour green paint onto a plastic plate.

2 Look at the photographs *above* to see how the trees are printed. Put the tip of your index finger lightly into the paint. Dab it six times in a tree shape on the paper. Make one print for the top, one for the trunk, and two on each side for branches. Make lots of trees on the paper. Let the paint dry. Glue a metallic star to the top of each tree.

MORE FINGERPRINT PROJECTS

BABY-FEET GIFT WRAP Pour red, blue, and yellow paint onto separate plastic plates. With your little finger curved, press the side of your hand into the paint. Press your hand on the paper to make a footprint. Make feet of one color wherever you wish, then add toes with your fingertip. To change colors, wash your hand, then repeat as above.

STATIONERY AND CARDS Turn plain cards and envelopes into happy greeting cards. Here we used slick paints to finger-paint designs. Then we also used them to write a greeting, draw lines, and make dots for highlights.

BOOKMARKS Your bookworm friends will love getting these bookmarks as gifts. Trace the patterns on page 21. Use carbon paper to transfer the designs to heavy paper. Cut out the shapes. Add finger dabs and other fancy strokes using slick paint.

**Finger-Painted
Bookmarks**

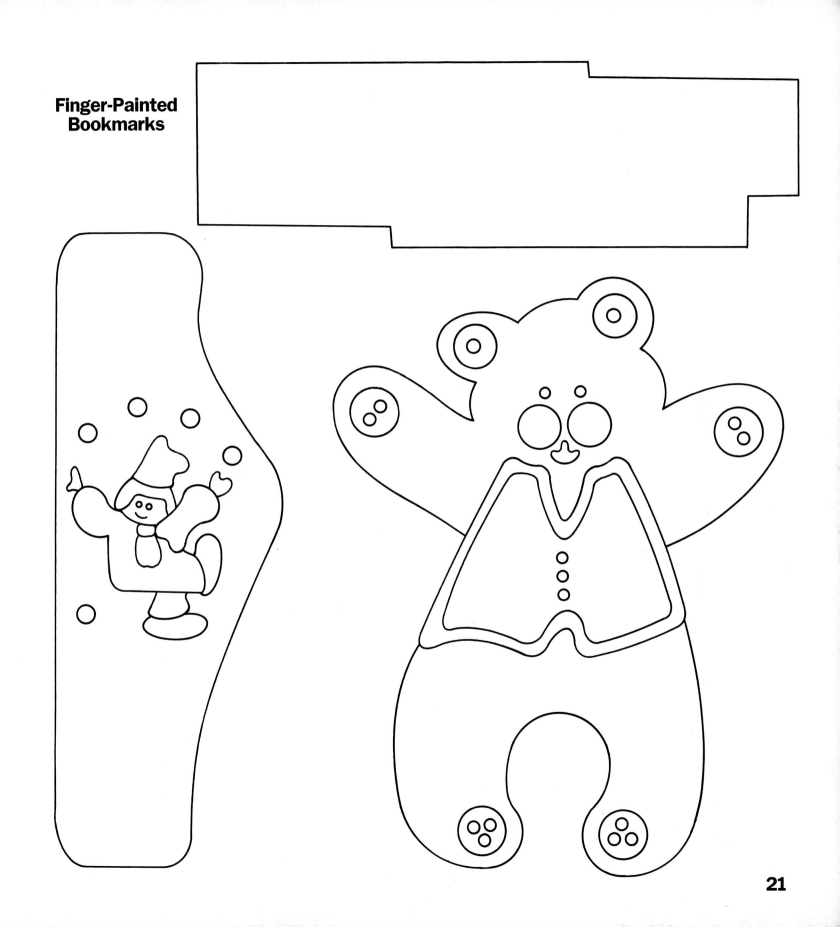

STICKS 'N' STONES

Gather a bundle of sticks or a pile of stones on a sunny afternoon walk. Your painterly talents will turn them into a cheerful bouquet of wands or a collection of bright and colorful paperweights.

TOOLBOX

- ▶ Bundle of sticks or a pile of rocks and stones
- ▶ Acrylic paints and slick-paint pens
- ▶ Paintbrush
- ▶ Extra-tacky crafts glue

1 Paint the entire surfaces of the rocks (top, sides, and bottom) with one color of acrylic paint. Let the paint dry.

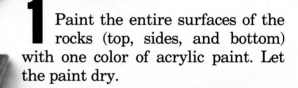

2 Paint one or more designs on one flat side of each rock. Let dry. Outline the design with slick paint.

3 You can glue stones together to make other shapes after all the pieces are dry. See the fish design, *left,* for an idea.

1 Get permission from your parents to use a handsaw to cut off the ends and the side branches of the sticks. You can paint over the bark or remove the bark before you begin to paint the sticks.

2 First paint entire sticks with one color of paint. Let dry. Paint stripes of bright colors around the sticks, allowing each color to dry before beginning with a new color.

SOAK

You'll look forward to rainy days after you've decorated your umbrella with lively designs. Here are colorful sponge-painted sailboats with wisps of paint to look like waves. See the next two pages for more sponge-painting ideas.

A SPONGE

TOOLBOX

- ▶ Felt-tip marker
- ▶ Sponges; scissors
- ▶ Tracing paper
- ▶ Old toothbrush
- ▶ Newspaper
- ▶ Umbrella
- ▶ Red, light green, yellow, and white slick-paint pens

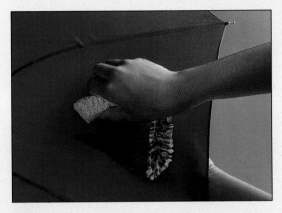

1 Trace the sailboat patterns on page 28 onto tracing paper. Cut out the patterns. Draw around the pattern shapes on the sponges using the felt-tip marker. Cut out the sponge shapes.

2 Cover your work area with newspaper to protect its surface.

3 Squeeze yellow paint onto one side of the boat sponge piece. Spread the paint evenly across the piece using a scrap piece of sponge. Use this same method to apply the paint to the sails using the colors indicated on the patterns.

4 Open the umbrella. Hold the sponge piece for the boat bottom by its sides and press it on the fabric. Print the sail pieces above it. Make a sailboat in each umbrella section. Allow the paint to dry.

5 To spatter-paint areas on the umbrella, apply a little white paint from a slick pen onto the bristles of the toothbrush. Hold the brush upside down over the area you want spattered and run your index finger across the bristles from front to back.

6 Use a white slick pen or any other color pen to make waves under the boats. Draw wild lines wherever you wish on the umbrella. Paint more details, such as dots, lines, and squiggles, onto the sailboats. Be sure to let the umbrella dry completely before you close it.

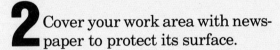

MORE SPONGE-PRINTING PROJECTS

SLICK SHIRTS Use the patterns on pages 28 and 29 to print shapes on all sizes and colors of shirts. The instructions for sponge-printing the umbrella on page 25 show you how to do it. For a friend, print hearts with slick-paint pens and add his or her name. Decorate a light blue shirt with wavy lines, dots, and the most unusual fish you can imagine. Or, for a nightshirt, create a mysterious night sky with glittering moons and shining stars.

HALLOWEEN BAGS Purchase colored gift bags and sponge-print them with Halloween motifs to create your own trick or treat bags. The pumpkin and ghost patterns are on pages 28 and 29. Use slick-paint pens to write a message or to add other decorative swirls. And for Christmas gift bags, there are patterns for a tree and bell on page 30.

Patterns for Sponge-Painted Umbrella, Slick Shirts, and Halloween Bags

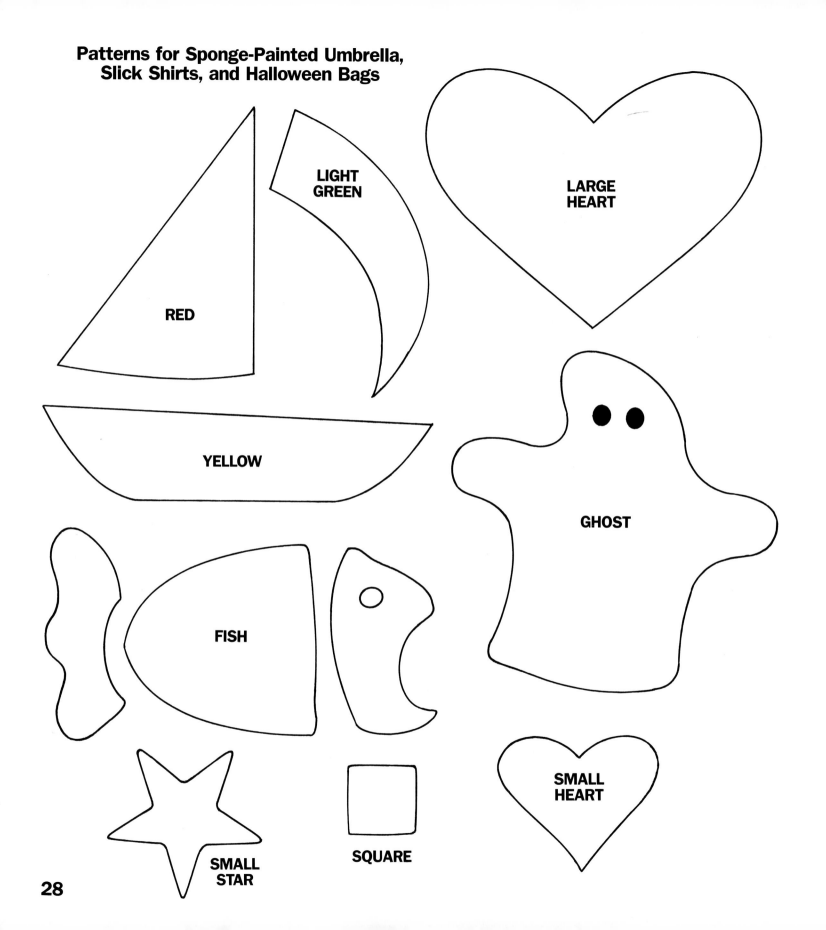

LIGHT GREEN

LARGE HEART

RED

YELLOW

GHOST

FISH

SMALL HEART

SMALL STAR

SQUARE

LARGE
STAR

JACK-O'-LANTERN

MOON

TULIP

APPLE

More Sponging Patterns

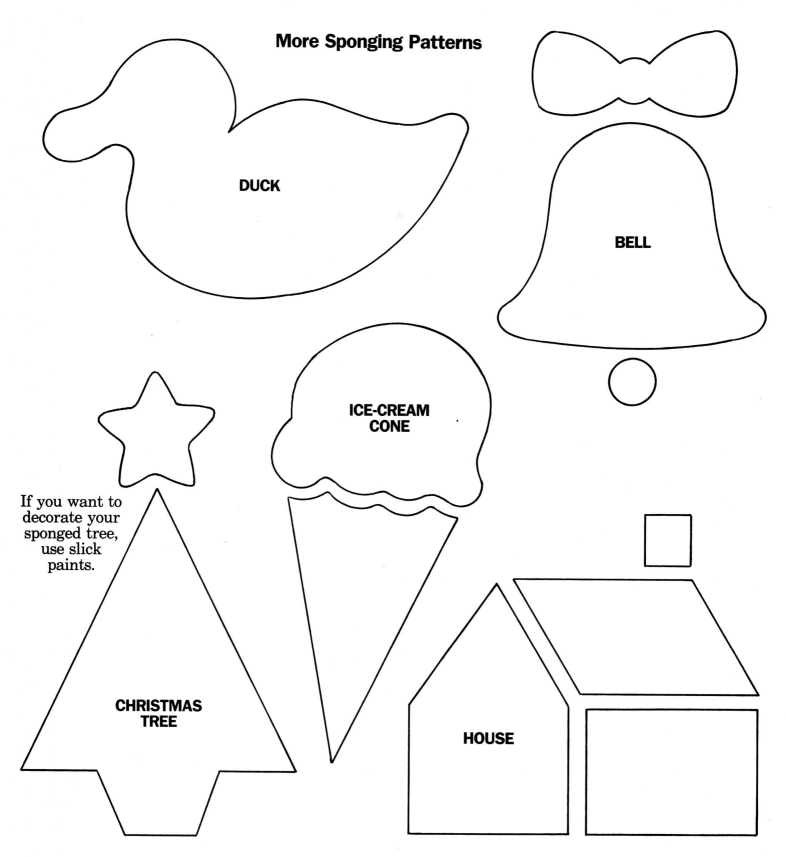

DUCK

BELL

ICE-CREAM
CONE

If you want to
decorate your
sponged tree,
use slick
paints.

CHRISTMAS
TREE

HOUSE

30

Design your own jewelry by tearing, cutting, painting, and pasting pieces of paper together. Follow our basic instructions, then turn the page for more terrific ideas.

TOOLBOX

▶ Heavy watercolor paper
▶ White construction paper
▶ Extra-tacky glue
▶ Slick-paint pens in iridescent colors
▶ Paintbrush
▶ Scissors
▶ Barrette clasp
▶ Pair of earring posts

1 For the barrette or earrings, tear a shape from the heavy water-color paper that is larger than the barrette clasp or the earring post.

2 For the barrette, use the heart pattern *below*. Cut it from white construction paper. Paint the heart with slick-paint pens, smoothing out the paint with your finger or brush. For both the barrette and the earrings, tear and paint small pieces of construction paper.

3 Place the cut and torn pieces on the barrette or the earring shapes as you wish, overlapping some of the pieces. Glue and let dry.

4 Use the slick pens to decorate the barrette or the earrings with lines, shapes, and dots.

Using extra-tacky glue, glue the clasp to the barrette or the posts to the earring shapes.

MORE TORN PAPER PROJECTS

GREETING CARDS

Make cards of various sizes and colors that fold over and fit purchased envelopes. Decorate them using the heart, stars, or dinosaur patterns on page 35. Tear more bits and pieces of painted papers. Arrange and glue the pieces on the cards. Use slick pens to add lines and dots for pizzazz.

CHRISTMAS ORNAMENTS

Follow the directions for the other collage projects to decorate these tree, bell, and ball trims. You can use the ornaments as gift tags, too. See pages 56 and 57 for more patterns.

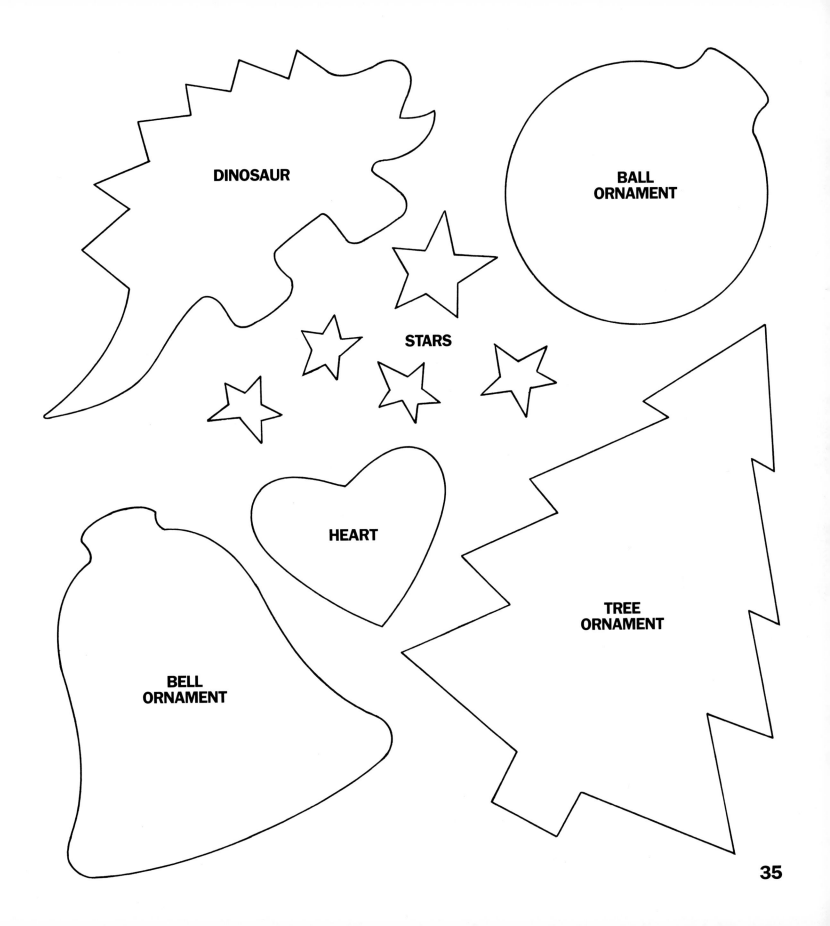

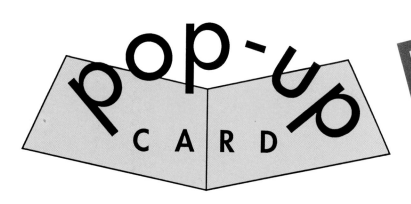

pop-up CARD

Here are step-by-step instructions for making the puppy card. By following these directions, you can make the chick card, too.

TOOLBOX

▶ Blue, black, brown, red, and white construction paper or Canson paper (available at art stores)
▶ Glue stick
▶ Crafts glue
▶ Tracing paper
▶ Carbon paper or graphite paper
▶ Ruler

1 Cut a 7x10-inch rectangle of blue paper. Fold it in half to measure 7x5 inches. Cut a 6½x9½-inch rectangle of white paper and fold it in half to measure 6½x4¾ inches.

2 Using tracing paper, trace the inside card pattern on page 38. Place the tracing on top of the *folded* white card. Use carbon paper to trace the cut and fold lines of the muzzle. Cut through both thicknesses of paper along the *cut* line only.

3 Open the card and pull up on the muzzle. Crease the paper along the fold lines. As you push up on the muzzle, it will pop out. Make a fold down the center of the muzzle that forces the muzzle to lie upward in the closed card.

36

4 Trace the puppy head, nose, tongue, and pupil patterns on page 38. Cut two pupils from black paper. Trace the remaining patterns onto folded colored papers, lining up the fold lines. Cut out these pieces, but do not cut along the fold lines.

5 Glue the head to the card, lining up the folds. Glue pupils, nose, and tongue in place. The top of the tongue is placed slightly under the muzzle—about ½ inch.

6 Smear glue from the glue stick on the wrong side of the white paper. Fasten the white paper to the inside of the folded blue card, lining up the center folds.

Trace the paw pattern on page 38. Cut two sets from black paper, and glue the paws to the front of the card using the photo at *left* as a guide.

POP-UP CHICK CARD Follow the instructions for the Puppy Card to make an Easter card using the patterns on page 39 and the photo *above* as a guide. For the egg shapes on the front of the card, use the marbleizing technique on pages 12 and 13 or use a pastel shade of construction paper.

37

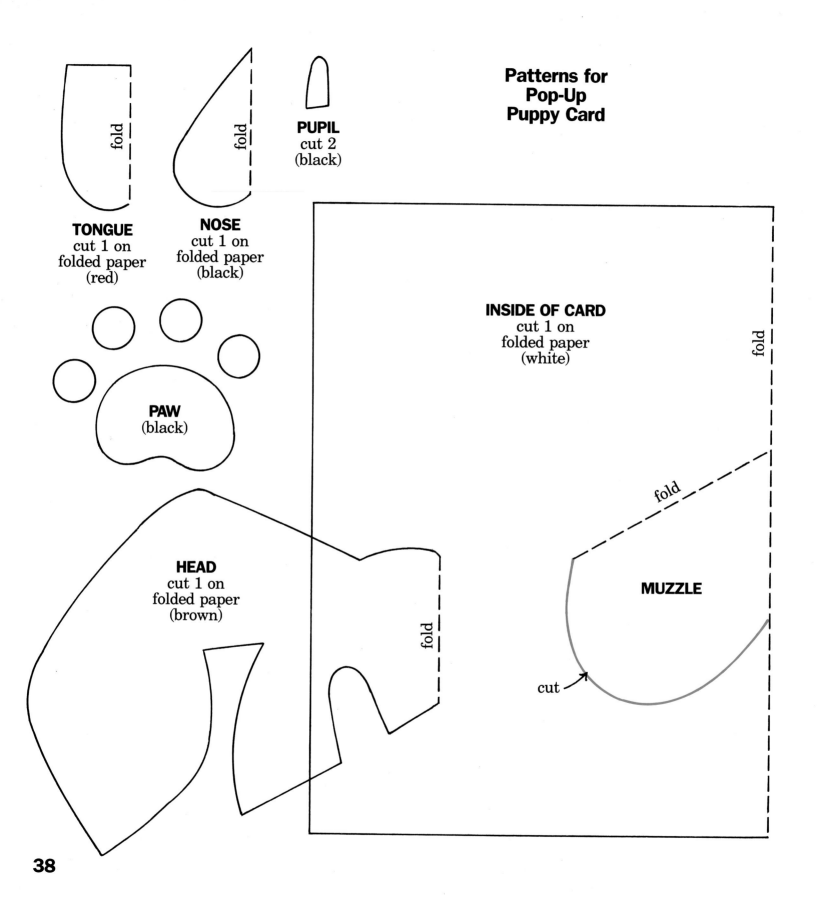

Patterns for Pop-Up Puppy Card

TONGUE cut 1 on folded paper (red)

fold

NOSE cut 1 on folded paper (black)

fold

PUPIL cut 2 (black)

PAW (black)

HEAD cut 1 on folded paper (brown)

fold

INSIDE OF CARD cut 1 on folded paper (white)

fold

fold

MUZZLE

cut

38

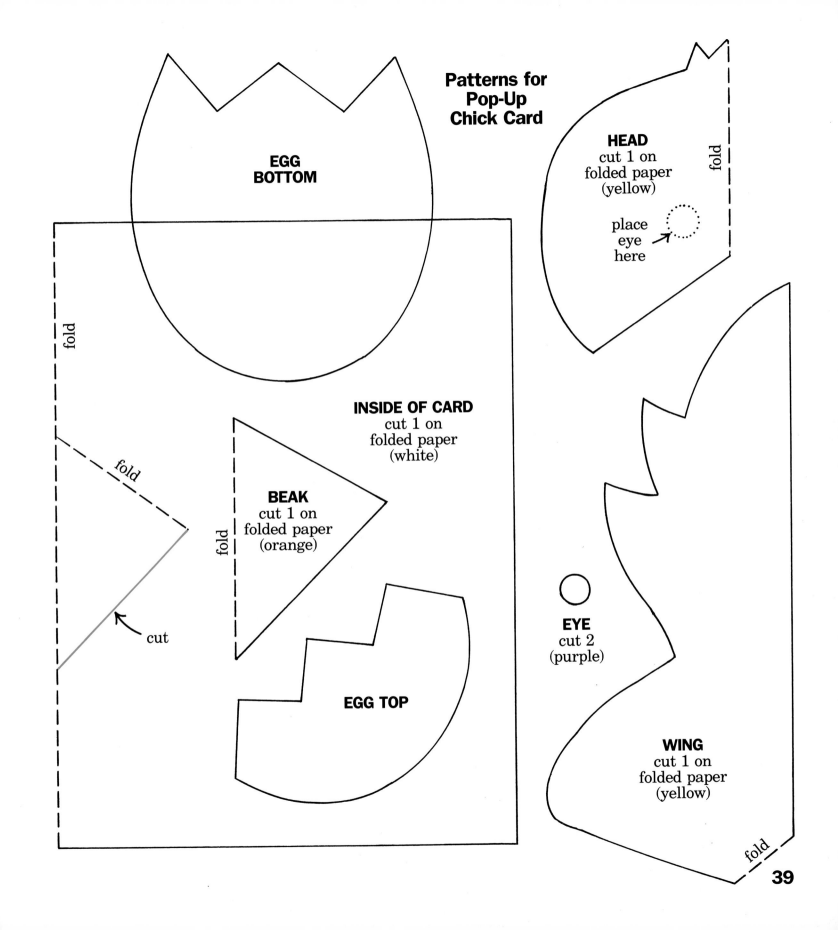

Patterns for Pop-Up Chick Card

EGG BOTTOM

fold

HEAD
cut 1 on
folded paper
(yellow)

fold

place eye here

INSIDE OF CARD
cut 1 on
folded paper
(white)

fold

cut

BEAK
cut 1 on
folded paper
(orange)

fold

EGG TOP

EYE
cut 2
(purple)

WING
cut 1 on
folded paper
(yellow)

fold

39

Tuneful Trims

Mus i cal an gels and peal ing bells, too.

Use glit ter and sheet mu sic, they are ea sy to do.

TOOLBOX

For all ornaments
- ▶ Several pages of sheet music
- ▶ Crafts glue
- ▶ Plastic tape
- ▶ Tracing paper
- ▶ Red or green glitter
- ▶ Saucer
- ▶ Aluminum foil
- ▶ Toothpick

For the bells
- ▶ Red, green, or gold heavy cotton thread
- ▶ Small jingle bells
- ▶ Large-eye needle

For the angels
- ▶ ¼-inch-wide green velvet ribbon
- ▶ 20-mm wooden beads
- ▶ 6-inch-diameter gold paper doilies
- ▶ Acrylic paints (See tip box on page 42.)
- ▶ Fine-tip paintbrush
- ▶ ¼-inch flat paintbrush

To make the bell

1 Trace the bell pattern on page 43 onto tracing paper and cut out the pattern. Place the pattern on the sheet music and draw around it. Cut out the shape.

2 Squeeze a small amount of glue onto the foil. Use a toothpick to run glue along the marked edge of the bell. Fasten the edges together to form a cone.

3 Pour the glitter into the saucer. Run a thin band of glue around the bottom edge of the bell. Working over the saucer, sprinkle glitter over the glue.

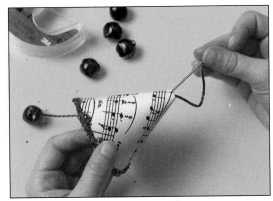

4 Cut an 8-inch-long piece of thread. Knot one end of the thread through the jingle bell. Put a small dab of glue on the knot. Trim the tail of the knot. Thread the other end into the needle. From the inside of the bell, push the needle up through the small opening at the top. Take the needle back through the opening, leaving a loop for hanging. Make sure the jingle bell dangles about ½ inch below the bottom of the bell. Tape the end of the thread to the inside of the bell to hold it in place.

5 Put a dab of glue at the top of the bell to keep the loop from slipping. Pinch the top edges together. Set the bell aside to dry.

TURN THE PAGE ▶

To make the angel ♪

TIPS FOR PAINTING THE ANGELS' HEADS

Use the flat brush to paint the entire bead the desired skin color. When the paint is dry, use the same brush to paint the hair. Use the fine-tip brush to paint the eyes, eyebrows, and mouth. The following paint colors can be used as a guide to paint the beads:

Use white for white faces.

Use red oxide mixed with raw umber to paint brown faces.

Use black to paint the eyes and eyebrows.

Use red to paint the mouths.

Use black, yellow, or raw sienna to paint the hair.

1 Using the angel body pattern on page 43, repeat steps 1–3 for making the bell on page 41. Clip off the point of the cone.

2 Use the face drawing on page 43 as a guide to paint the head on the bead. See the tips at *left* for colors.

3 Cut a 10-inch-long piece of ribbon and fold it in half. To make a hanger, tie an overhand knot about 1 inch from the fold.

4 Push the ribbon ends through the bead and into the top of the cone. Tape the ribbon ends to the insides of the cone.

5 For the wings, fold a doily in half, matching designs. Using the diagram on page 43, cut out the center top of the doily. Cut a 2-inch slit in the center bottom of the folded doily as shown on the diagram.

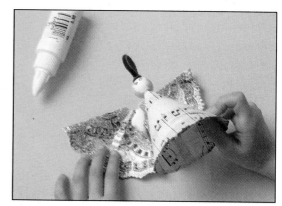

6 Flare the top fold of the wings upward and make small folds for pleats as shown on the diagram. Glue the pleated areas to the back of the angel body below the head. When dry, open the wings slightly, pleating or gathering some areas for a three-dimensional look.

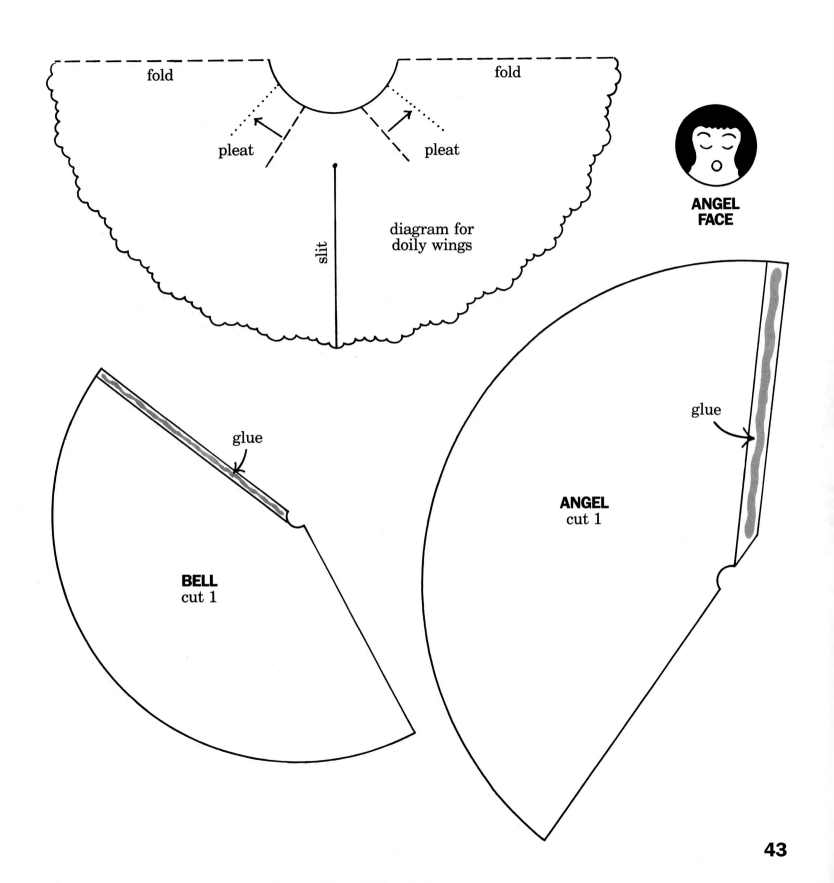

fold

fold

pleat

pleat

slit

diagram for
doily wings

**ANGEL
FACE**

glue

glue

ANGEL
cut 1

BELL
cut 1

The Write Stuff

NOTEBOOK COVERS

Use unusual papers, stickers, and paints to cover and decorate spiral notebooks.

TOOLBOX

- ▶ Spiral notebook
- ▶ Two contrasting colors of paper to cover the notebook
- ▶ Ruler
- ▶ Glue stick

1 Measure and cut four pieces of paper that are each ½ inch larger than the notebook on all sides. Cut two from one color for the outside front and back covers and two from the other color for the inside covers.

2 Fold under ½ inch of the paper edge that fits below the spirals for the outside front cover. Then fold under the two side edges so these edges are even with the edges of the notebook.

44

3 Fold the bottom edge around to the back side of the cover. Use the glue stick to fasten this flap to the notebook. Keep the side edges folded on the front side.

4 With the notebook open, fold under ½ inch of the paper that fits along the spirals for the inside front cover. Fold under the bottom edge so it is almost even with the bottom of the notebook.

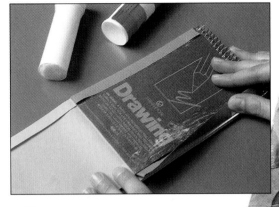

5 Close the notebook and flip back the outside paper cover only. Fold the inside cover edges to the front of the book. Use the glue stick to fasten the flaps to the notebook. Fold the outside cover back in place.

6 Repeat steps 2-5 to cover the back of the notebook.

7 From the paper that was used for the inside covers, cut a binding strip 3 to 4 inches wide and 1 inch longer than the length of the spiral. Fold under ½ inch on each of the short ends so that the strip measures as long as the spiral.

Tuck the strip behind the front and back covers over the spiral. Decorate the cover of the book as you like.

COVER IDEAS

You can decorate your own paper for covers using the marbleizing technique on pages 12 and 13, or the fingerprint ideas on pages 18 and 19. Use gift wrap, brown paper wrap, or newspaper. More fun is in store when you begin to decorate the covers. Use stickers, slick-paint pens, adhesive-backed letters and numbers, or any materials that will stick to your cover through lots of wear and tear.

MAP MANIA

Old road maps can be used in surprising ways. Here we show you how to cover a lampshade with a map. And there are more ideas on the next two pages.

TOOLBOX

- Purchased smooth-sided lampshade
- Ruler
- One or two large maps
- 1 yard of ⅛-inch-wide ribbon
- Crafts glue
- Strand of yarn
- Paper punch with ⅛-inch hole
- Large-eye sewing needle

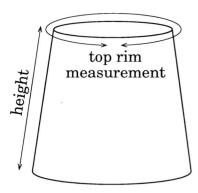

height

top rim measurement

1 Referring to the drawing *below left*, measure the height of the shade and add ¾ inch. Measure around the top rim of the shade. Multiply this number by three.

2 From the map, cut out a rectangle the size of your measurements. If your map isn't large enough, glue two maps together.

3 With the ruler and pencil and the wrong side of the map facing you, lightly draw lines 1 inch apart along the length of the map. Fold and firmly crease along each marked line.

4 To make the accordion pleats, line up and match the first two folds and crease the paper under the fold. Continue to match up the folds and crease the pleats along the length of the map.

When all the pleats are made, overlap the short edges and glue them together to form a tube.

5 Use the paper punch to punch holes in the center of each pleat along one edge only (this will be the top edge of the shade). Try to keep the holes ¼ inch from the top edge. Thread the ribbon through the punched holes.

6 Run a line of glue around the top edge of the purchased shade. Place the shade on the lamp. Slip the pleated shade over the purchased shade and pull up the ribbon so the pleats fit along the rim. Tie a knot in the ribbon and then tie a bow. Space the pleats evenly along the rim of the shade. Let the glue dry.

7 Run a line of glue around the bottom rim of the purchased shade and spread the glue to prevent it from dripping. Tie a strand of yarn around the lower half of the shade to pull in the pleats. Space the pleats evenly along the bottom rim. Let the glue dry. Remove the yarn.

MORE MAP MANIA PROJECTS

MAP CASE To make a storage case for road maps, take apart a lunch bag and use it for a pattern. Draw around the pattern on the map and cover the map with adhesive-backed clear vinyl. Cut, fold, and glue the map into the bag shape, adding a flap and some buttons to hold the flap closed. Fasten 1-inch adhesive-backed letters.

TRAVEL DIARY Turn to pages 58 and 59 to learn how to make a book with an old map as the cover. Take the book along on vacations to jot down daily events. Jazz it up by tying beads on the ends of the binding threads for decorations.

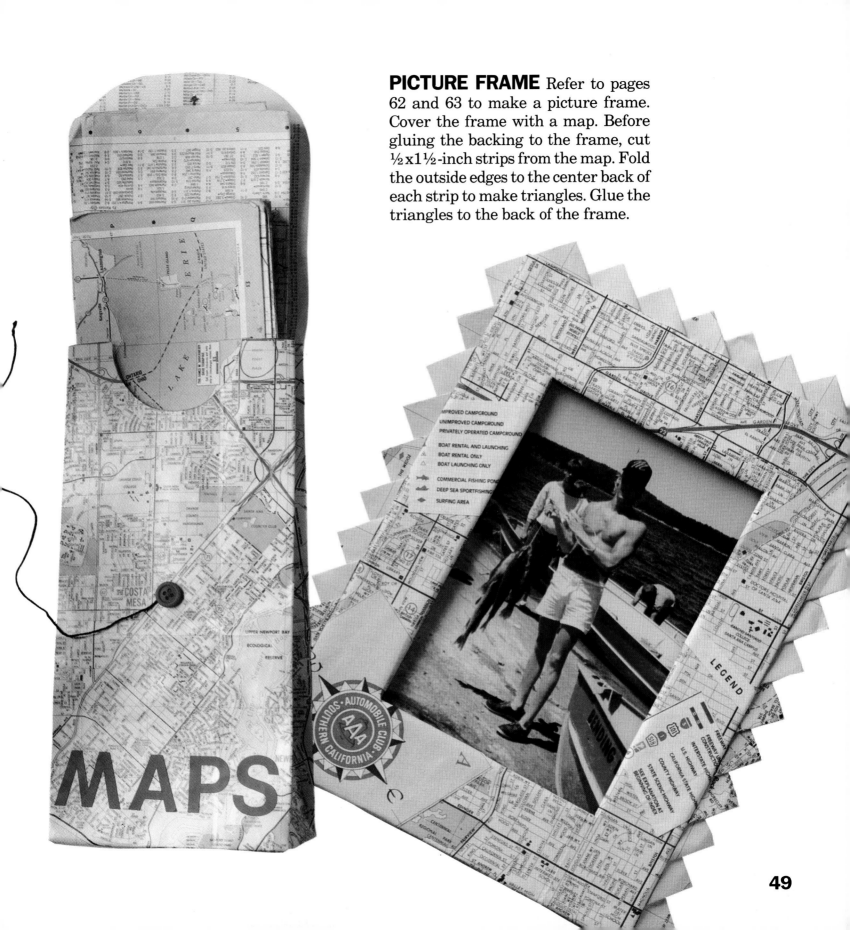

PICTURE FRAME Refer to pages 62 and 63 to make a picture frame. Cover the frame with a map. Before gluing the backing to the frame, cut ½ x1½-inch strips from the map. Fold the outside edges to the center back of each strip to make triangles. Glue the triangles to the back of the frame.

STACK THE DECK

With ordinary playing cards and some colorful ribbon, you can make our version of the Jacob's Ladder folk art toy.

TOOLBOX

▲ 15 playing cards
▲ Tacky glue
▲ One 44-inch length of ¼-inch-wide red ribbon
▲ Two 44-inch lengths of ¼-inch-wide blue ribbon

1 To apply glue to the cards as you follow these project instructions, squeeze glue around the edges of a card. Then use another card to spread the glue all over the first card, just like you spread butter on bread.

2 To begin, spread glue on one card. Glue the end of one red ribbon to the top of the card. Glue the ends of the blue ribbons at the bottom of the same card. Notice the placements of the ribbons at both ends of the card. Fasten a card on top of the glued one. Line up the card edges.

3 Spread glue on another card. Take the red ribbon back across the *top* of the glued pair of cards. Leaving a tiny space between the cards, fasten only the red ribbon to the center of this glued card.

TURN THE PAGE ▶

FRONT OF JACOB'S LADDER

The photo at *left* shows the top side of the arrangement of the seven cards and ribbons when the ladder is complete. It is important to note that when a ribbon or ribbons are glued between two cards, the ribbon also will show on the front and back of the same card.

8 Repeat steps 4, 5, 6, and 7.

9 Repeat Step 4.

10 Spread glue on another card. Take the blue ribbons across the *back* of the glued pair of cards. Glue the blue ribbons to the next card. Trim the ends of the ribbons 1 inch from the bottom of the card.

11 Fasten a card on top of this card, keeping the red ribbon free. Line up the card edges.

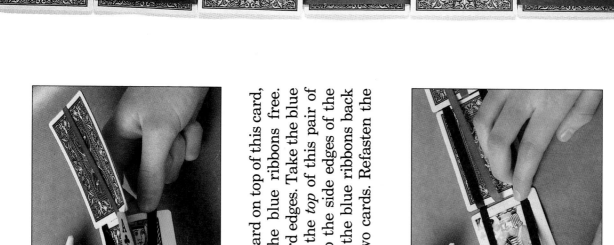

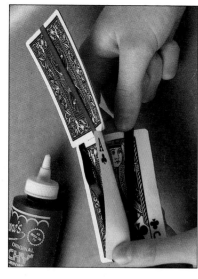

4 Fasten a card on top of this card, keeping the blue ribbons free. Line up the card edges. Take the blue ribbons across the *top* of this pair of cards. Open up the side edges of the cards and run the blue ribbons back between the two cards. Refasten the card edges.

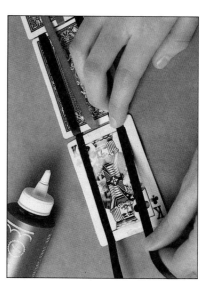

5 Spread glue on another card. Take the blue ribbons across the back of the glued pair of cards. Glue the blue ribbons to the next card.

12 Bring the red ribbon across the *back* of the glued pair of cards. Open up the glued cards and run the red ribbon between the two cards. Trim the ribbon end. Refasten the card edges.

BACK SIDE OF JACOB'S LADDER

The photo at *left* shows the back side of the cards and ribbons when the ladder is complete. On the back side of the ladder, we always put the glue on the face of the cards. This made it easy to line up the blue ribbons when we glued them to the cards.

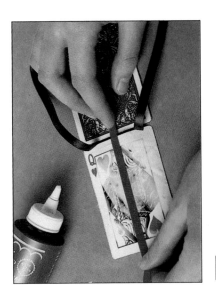

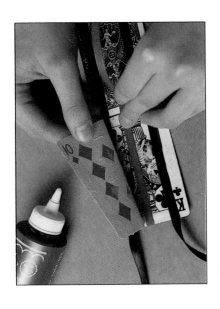

6 Fasten a card to the top of this card, keeping the red ribbon free. Take the red ribbon across the *back* of the bottom of the glued cards. Open up the glued cards and run the red ribbon back between the two cards. Refasten the card edges.

7 Spread glue on another card. Take the red ribbon back across the *top* of the glued pair of cards. Glue this ribbon to the next card.

53

STRINGS AND THINGS

Materials that you can find around the house are all you need for these ornaments.

TOOLBOX

► Tracing paper
► Construction paper
► Ballpoint pen
► Waxed paper
► Jar of acrylic gloss medium and varnish
► Scraps of yarns, strings, or threads
► Crafts glue
► Paintbrush
► Trims such as beads, sequins, pom-poms, and glitter

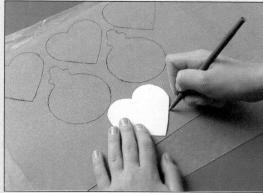

1 Trace patterns of your choice on pages 56 and 57. Cut out the patterns. Draw around the patterns on the construction paper using the ballpoint pen.

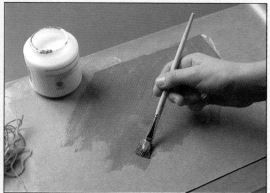

2 Cover the work area with waxed paper. Turn the construction paper over so the drawn patterns face the waxed paper. Paint the entire surface of the construction paper with the gloss medium and varnish.

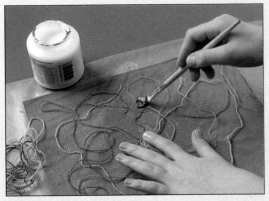

3 While the varnish is still wet, swirl string, yarn, or thread over the paper. Use the brush and the gloss medium and varnish to dab along the string to fasten it to the paper. You can sprinkle glitter over the wet surface. Let the paper dry.

4 Turn the paper over and cut out the drawn shapes.

5 Glue more trims to the designs using the ornaments shown here for ideas.

Patterns for Strings and Things

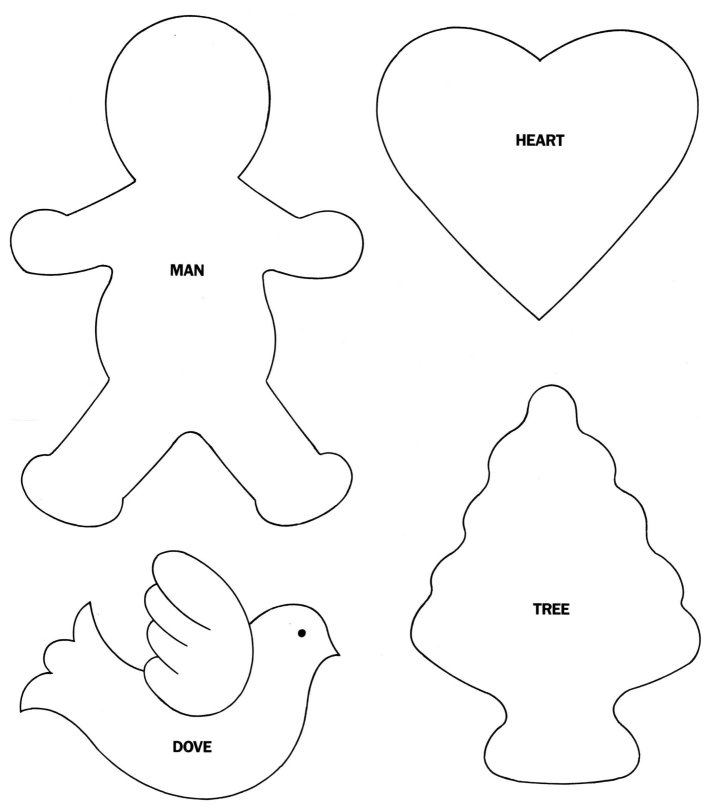

MAN

HEART

DOVE

TREE

WHALE

Make other Strings and Things
shapes by drawing around cookie cutters.

STOCKING

BEAR

Ties That Bind

Make your own diary, sketch book, and photo album using imaginative materials to decorate their covers and colorful threads for bindings.

TOOLBOX

▶ Two matching picture frame backing boards for book covers
▶ Cardboard scrap for two binding strips (use the back of a tablet)
▶ Two different papers to decorate covers and binding strips
▶ Paper for pages
▶ Rubber cement
▶ Two spring paper clips
▶ Ruler
▶ Hammer
▶ Nail; scrap piece of wood
▶ Sewing needle
▶ Colorful thread

1 For the front and back outside covers, cut two pieces of paper that are ½ inch larger than all sides of the boards. Use rubber cement to fasten the paper to the boards. Glue the edges to the backs of the boards.

2 Cut two binding strips from the cardboard that are about 1 inch wide and the length of the spine edge of the book.

COVER PAPERS

You can use just about any kind of paper to cover your book. Below, we used marbled paper (see pages 12 and 13). On the middle book, we covered the paper with cellophane and sprinkled confetti and glitter trims behind it. Origami papers are cut into perfect squares when you buy them. Use these to make a design of squares and rectangles as shown on page 60.

3 Cut two strips of paper that are ½ inch larger than all edges of the binding strips. Glue the paper strips to the cardboard strips.

4 For the hinges, cut four strips of paper that are ½ inch shorter than the book's spine edge and about 3 inches wide. Glue two paper pieces together to make one paper hinge that is double in thickness. Then make another hinge.

5 Glue one side of each hinge to the back of each binding strip.

Leaving a gap of about ⅛ inch between the binding strip and the back of the board, glue the other side of the hinge to the back of each of the book covers.

TURN THE PAGE ▶

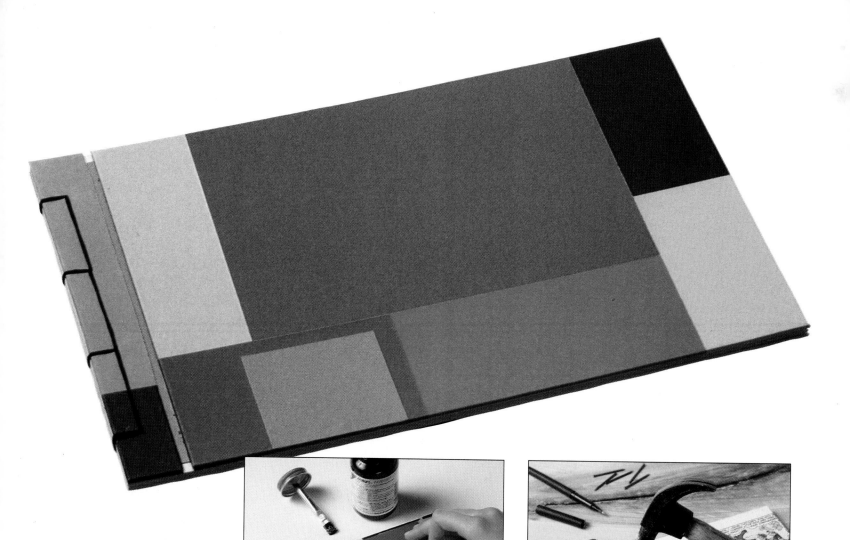

CUTTING THE PAPER You may need to trim the paper for the pages to fit your book. Make sure you cut it so it fits the full surface of the cover board plus the binding strip. If you don't have a paper cutter at home, use one at your school. Ask a teacher to help you cut the paper.

6 For the inside covers, cut two pieces of paper that are ¼ inch smaller on all sides than the cover boards. Glue these to the backs of the covers, covering the hinges.

7 Cut paper for the pages so it fits your book. See the paper-cutting tip at *left*.

8 Assemble the book using the spring clips to hold it together. Mark three to four dots equal distance apart on the front cover binding strip. Laying the book on a scrap piece of wood, use a hammer and nail to make holes at the dots all the way through the book.

60

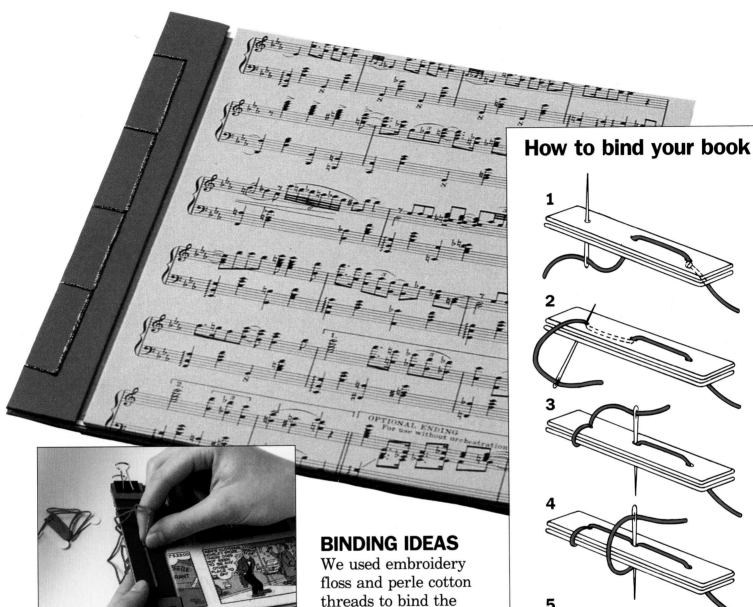

How to bind your book

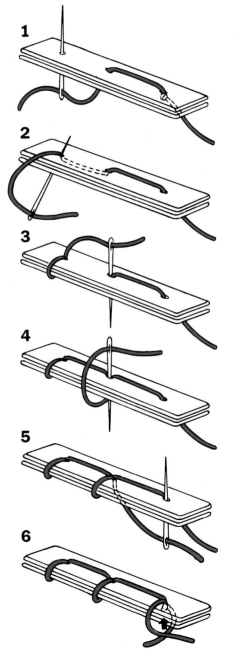

1
2
3
4
5
6

BINDING IDEAS

We used embroidery floss and perle cotton threads to bind the books. But you can use ribbons, strings, cords, metallic thread, and even an extra-long shoelace. If you use a shoelace, you can use the plastic tip at the end to lace it through the holes.

9 Thread a needle with a double strand of thread, making a knot 4 inches from the ends. The double length of thread should measure four times the length of the book's bound edge.

Referring to the diagrams, *right*, follow steps 1–6 to bind your book. At the end of Step 6, knot the tail ends together and clip the ends.

JIGSAW JUNK

Don't throw away that puzzle with the missing pieces! Instead, turn it into colorful objects such as these picture frames. On the next two pages we show you other ways to use those leftover pieces.

1 Use the glue to fasten the puzzle pieces to the mat frame with the opening. Layer the pieces until the mat board doesn't show. Set it aside.

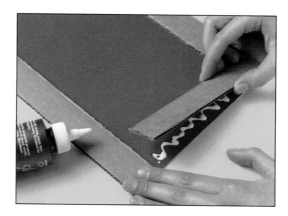

2 From corrugated cardboard cut strips to fit along two sides and across the bottom edge of the mat without the opening. Glue the strips to the mat. Once assembled, the uncovered edge will form a slot for slipping a photo into the frame.

3 To cover the backing mat, cut a piece of wrapping paper 1½ inches larger on all sides than the backing. To finish the top edge of the paper, cut it up to the mat and even with the inside edges of the cardboard strips. Use rubber cement to glue this flap to the board. Glue the other three edges to the cardboard strips.

4 Trace the frame support and fastener patterns on page 66 and cut them out. Draw around the patterns on the cardboard and cut them out. Cut wrapping paper 1 inch larger on all sides than the cardboard pieces. Use rubber cement to glue the paper on one side and over the edges of these pieces. Then cut and glue a piece of wrapping paper to fit over the uncovered side of the frame support. Do not cover the back of the fastener piece.

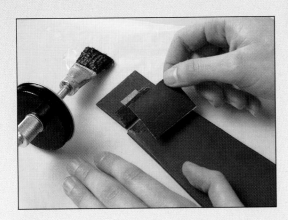

5 To make a hinge, cut two fastener pieces from wrapping paper. Glue these pieces together. Glue one half of the hinge to the back side of the fastener piece and the other half to the back side of the support, spacing the two pieces about ⅛ inch apart.

6 Glue the puzzle-covered mat to the backing mat. Center the assembled stand on the back of the backing and glue *only the fastener* to the board. Let dry.

Center the ribbon on the back of the support piece and use glue to fasten it in place. Adjust the ribbon for standing. Glue the ribbon to the back of the backing. Trim the ribbon ends.

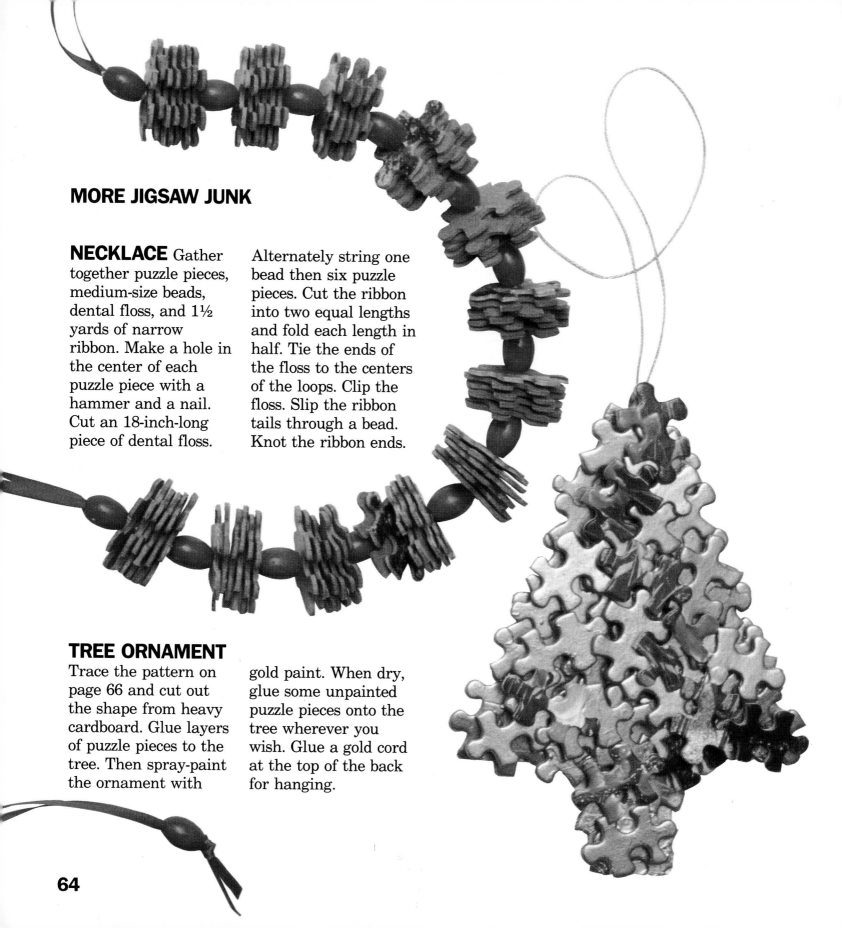

MORE JIGSAW JUNK

NECKLACE Gather together puzzle pieces, medium-size beads, dental floss, and 1½ yards of narrow ribbon. Make a hole in the center of each puzzle piece with a hammer and a nail. Cut an 18-inch-long piece of dental floss. Alternately string one bead then six puzzle pieces. Cut the ribbon into two equal lengths and fold each length in half. Tie the ends of the floss to the centers of the loops. Clip the floss. Slip the ribbon tails through a bead. Knot the ribbon ends.

TREE ORNAMENT

Trace the pattern on page 66 and cut out the shape from heavy cardboard. Glue layers of puzzle pieces to the tree. Then spray-paint the ornament with gold paint. When dry, glue some unpainted puzzle pieces onto the tree wherever you wish. Glue a gold cord at the top of the back for hanging.

CHRISTMAS WREATH Trace the wreath pattern on page 67 and cut out the shape from heavy cardboard. Glue layers of puzzle pieces over the circle, allowing pieces to extend over the edges. Glue some silk or plastic greens and a bright ribbon bow at the top. Use extra-tacky glue to fasten a string hanger on the back of the wreath.

Patterns for Puzzle Projects

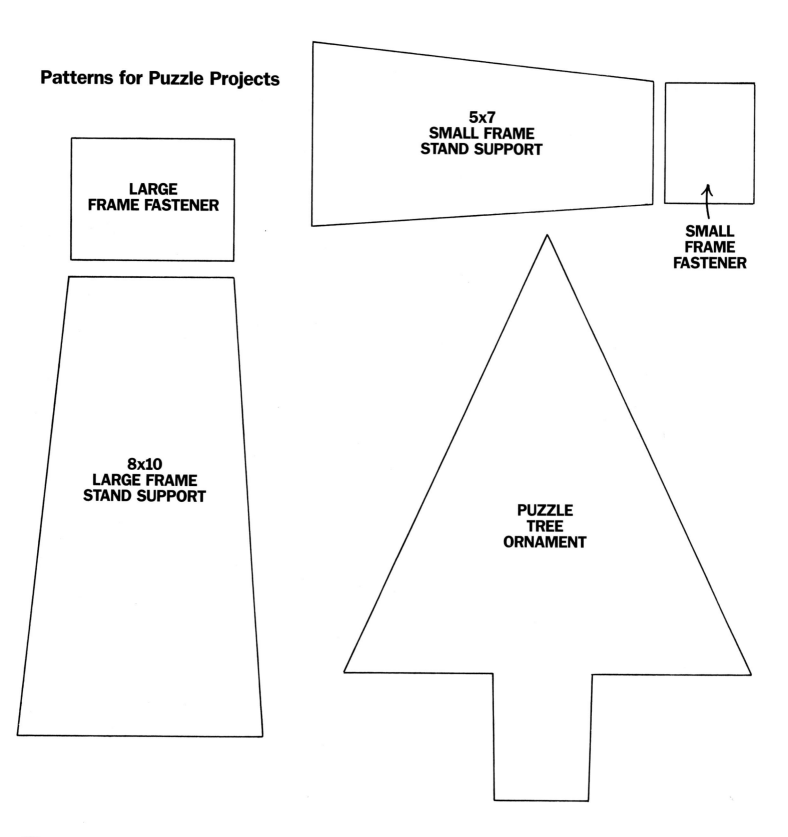

LARGE
FRAME FASTENER

5x7
SMALL FRAME
STAND SUPPORT

SMALL
FRAME
FASTENER

8x10
LARGE FRAME
STAND SUPPORT

PUZZLE
TREE
ORNAMENT

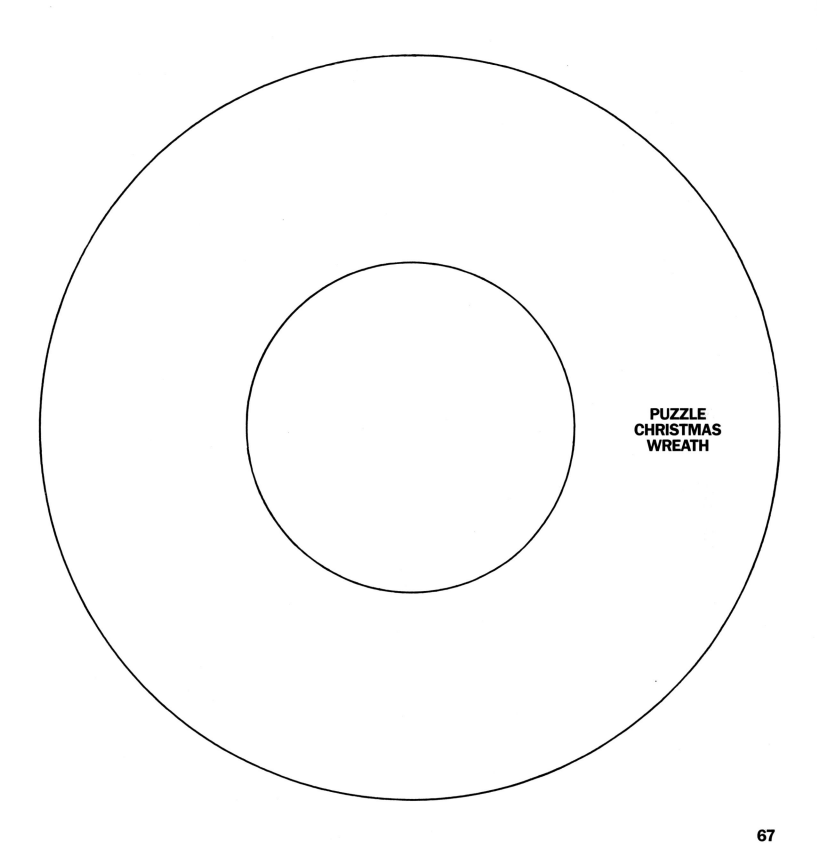

PUZZLE
CHRISTMAS
WREATH

MARDI GRAS MASKS

You may not scare anyone with these paper plate masks, but they are fun to make. The instructions show you how to make this red mask. There are more mask ideas on the following two pages.

68

TOOLBOX

- ▶ Red, gold, or other colorful 7-inch-diameter deep-dish paper plates
- ▶ Tracing paper
- ▶ Hole punch
- ▶ Gold or silver glitter
- ▶ Scissors
- ▶ Crafts glue
- ▶ Ballpoint pen
- ▶ Gold star stickers
- ▶ Gold curling ribbon
- ▶ Beads or other decorative trims of your choice
- ▶ Rubber band mask holder or 18-inch-long ¼-inch-diameter dowel

1 Trace the pattern for the red mask on page 72. Cut out the pattern. Lay the traced pattern over a red paper plate and draw around the shape. Cut out the shape from the paper plate. Notice how the pattern fits over the sloped edges of the plate.

2 Cut the eyebrows from the edges of a gold plate. Clip the edges to fringe the eyebrows. Glue the eyebrows on the back side at the top of the mask.

3 Run a band of glue around the eyes or other areas of the mask that you want to decorate with glitter. Sprinkle glitter over the glue. Shake the excess glitter off the mask. Let the glue dry.

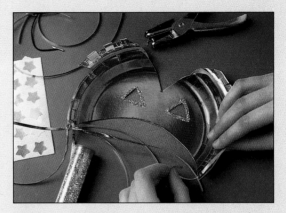

4 Punch holes in the bottom corners of the mask. Cut six strands of gold curling ribbon that are about 12 inches long. Evenly pull three ribbons through each punched hole. Curl three of the ribbon pieces in each corner with the blades of the scissors. String beads on the ends of the uncurled ribbon pieces. Tie overhand knots below the beads to hold them in place. Fasten gold stickers or other trims to the mask.

5 You can either punch holes in the sides of the masks and fasten a rubber band mask holder or glue a dowel to one side for a handle.

MORE MARDI GRAS MASKS

CHOOSING PAPER PLATES

Paper plates are ideal for making masks. The 7-inch-diameter size will fit perfectly across your face. Although we used metallic colored plates for these masks, you can use any kind of paper plate. Try coloring or painting a plain white paper plate. Then add sparkle by decorating it with a variety of trims.

DAZZLING DETAILS Use the curved rim of plates of different colors to add more playfulness to your mask, or trim it with colored construction paper. Glue on beads, sequins, buttons, crepe papers, ribbons, pom-poms, or other items to make it match your costume.

Patterns for Paper-Plate Masks

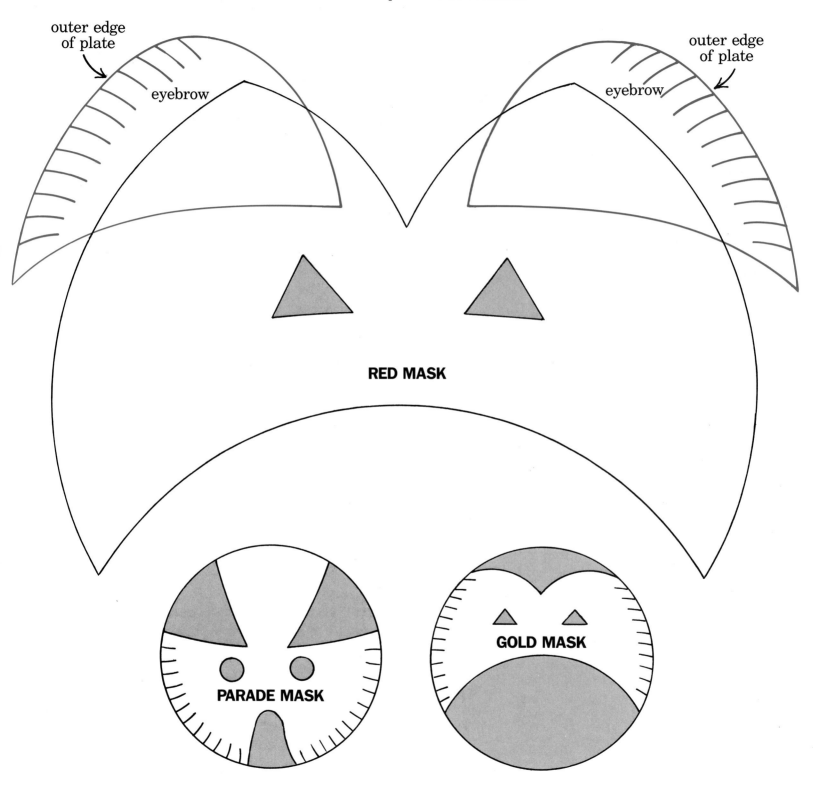

outer edge of plate

eyebrow

outer edge of plate

eyebrow

RED MASK

PARADE MASK

GOLD MASK

FISH MASK

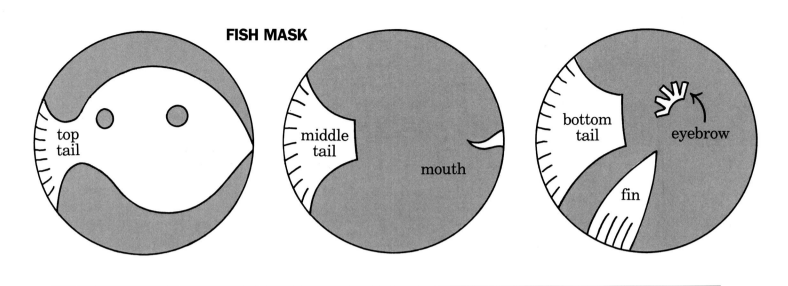

FLOWER MASK

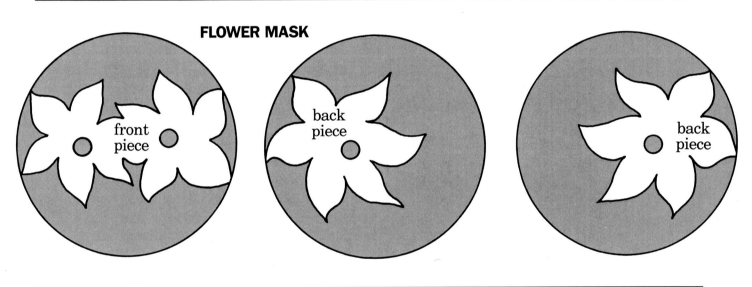

SUN MASK

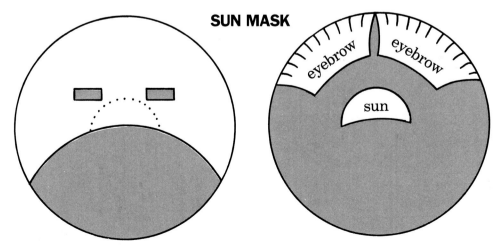

73

PAPER PUNCH PORKERS

Glue punched paper dots to blown-out eggs to make the barnyard pigs on this page or the menagerie of critters on the next two pages.

TOOLBOX

▶ Eggs
▶ Straight pin
▶ Red and pink construction paper
▶ Paper punch
▶ Tacky glue
▶ Toothpick
▶ Tracing paper
▶ 7-mm glue eyes
▶ Pink pipe cleaner
▶ Fine-tipped black marker

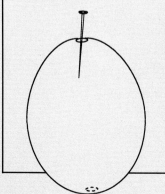

1 Wash the eggs in warm soapy water, rinse, and dry.

Referring to the egg diagram *at left,* poke a hole in the top and bottom of the egg using the straight pin. Make each hole approximately ⅛ inch in diameter.

Place your mouth over one hole and blow hard. The egg contents will come out the other hole. Rinse out the eggshell and set it aside to dry.

2 Punch lots of dots from folded pink construction paper using the paper punch.

3 Squeeze a small amount of glue around the narrow end of the egg. Spread the glue around with the toothpick. Fasten dots to the glued area. *Do not cover the hole.*

4 Squeeze more glue onto the egg and spread it with the toothpick. Fasten dots to the glued area. Continue adding glue and fastening dots until the egg is covered. Set the egg aside to allow the glue to dry.

5 Use tracing paper to trace the leg, nose, nose circle, mouth, and ear patterns on page 78. Cut out the patterns. From pink construction paper, trace and cut out four legs, one nose and nose circle, and two ears. Cut one mouth from red paper.

74

7 Wrap the nose strip around a pencil and glue the edges together; let glue dry. Slip the nose off the pencil. Glue the nose circle to one end of the nose. Glue the nose to the center of the wide end of the egg. Crease the mouth and glue it below the nose. Use the fine-tipped black marker to draw nostrils at the end of the nose.

6 Wrap each leg strip around a pencil. Glue the edges together to make four tubes. Slip the legs off the pencil. Glue the legs to the underside of the pig body.

8 Glue on eyes. Draw eyebrows above the eyes. Glue ears to the head above the eyebrows. Curl the tips of the ears around the pencil.

9 Twist a 2-inch-long piece of pipe cleaner around a pencil. Slip the curled pipe cleaner off the pencil. Dab glue onto one end and insert it into the hole at the tail end of the egg.

MORE PAPER PUNCH CRITTERS

Now that you've made the pig, you can make the critters here, or create some of your own designs. Blow out more eggs and you're ready to begin. The patterns for the body parts are on page 78.

BUMBLEBEE Use black and yellow dots to make the bumblebee body. Add black wings, eyes, a mouth, and a 1-inch-long stinger at the tail end. For antennae, push two straight pins with black glass heads into the top of the head.

LADYBUG Punch out red and black dots to make the ladybug body. Use a pin to make holes for the pipe cleaner legs and antennae. Glue on the mouth, feet, and eyes.

LAMB Use black dots to make circles for the face and tail areas on both ends of the egg. Cut off the cotton ends of cotton swabs and glue these over the body. Make black legs and ears. Glue them to the body. Add glue-on eyes and paper strips for the mouth.

GOLDFISH Glue orange dots to the egg. Use patterns to make a felt tail and the top and side fin pieces. Glue the matching pieces together. Then glue them to the fish body. Twist small pipe cleaners into circles for eyes, and glue purchased eyes to the circles. Make a diamond-shaped pipe cleaner for the mouth.

PENGUIN Cover the body with black and white dots. Use the patterns to make the paper hat, wings, and stand. Roll the hat crown to make a tube and glue the edges. Glue the brim and top to the tube. Make the vest from black and white felt. Make the mouth from orange paper.

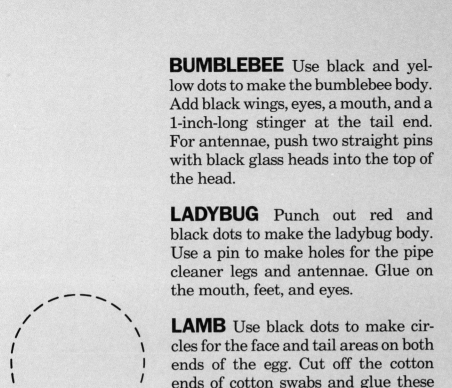

Patterns for Decorated Eggs

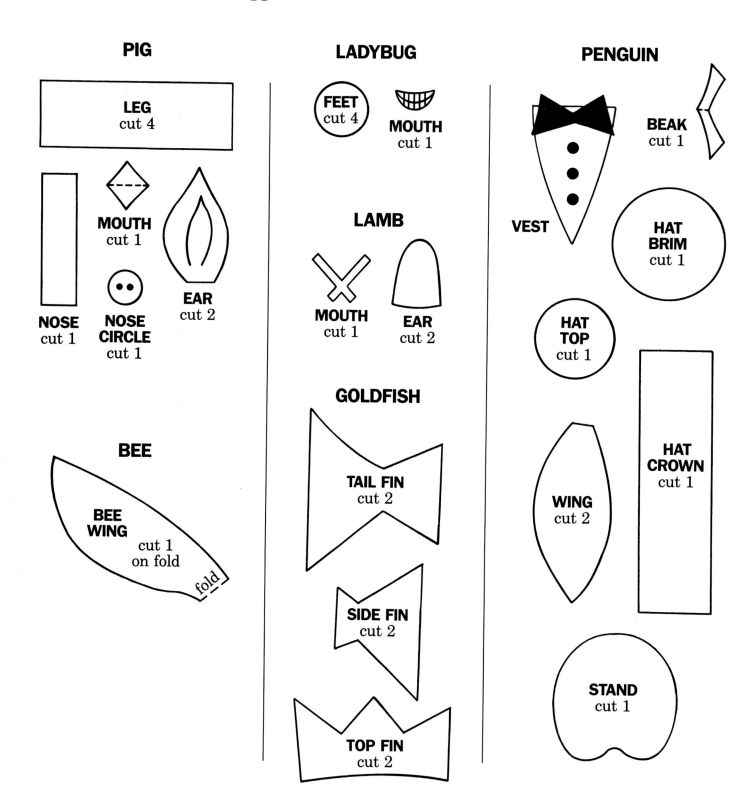

PIG

LEG
cut 4

MOUTH
cut 1

NOSE
cut 1

NOSE
CIRCLE
cut 1

EAR
cut 2

BEE

BEE
WING
cut 1
on fold

fold

LADYBUG

FEET
cut 4

MOUTH
cut 1

LAMB

MOUTH
cut 1

EAR
cut 2

GOLDFISH

TAIL FIN
cut 2

SIDE FIN
cut 2

TOP FIN
cut 2

PENGUIN

BEAK
cut 1

VEST

HAT
BRIM
cut 1

HAT
TOP
cut 1

WING
cut 2

HAT
CROWN
cut 1

STAND
cut 1

SHAPE, SCULPT, AND BUILD

TOOLBOX

▶ Balloons
▶ Liquid starch
▶ Old newspapers
▶ Old cake or pie tin
▶ String
▶ Paper or plastic cup
▶ Colored tissue paper
▶ Can of flat white spray paint
▶ Jar of gloss medium and varnish
▶ Paintbrush

Paper-mache over blown-up balloons makes baskets. Use tissue papers for the last layer to add the color. See the next two pages for more ideas.

1 Tear newspapers into 1-inch-wide strips that are 2 to 3 inches long. Blow up the balloon and tie the end with an overhand knot.

2 Pour starch into the pie tin. Cover the balloon with newspaper strips that have been dipped into the starch. After the balloon is covered with this layer, add a second layer. Overlap the strips and completely cover the balloon, except for the knotted end. Tie a string above the knot of the balloon. Hang the balloon in a cool, dry area to dry overnight. Add more strips, if necessary, and let these strips dry.

3 Snip the knotted end from the balloon, let the air escape, and remove the balloon. Let the paper ball dry for a few more hours.

4 Cut 1 inch off the top of the plastic cup to use for the base. Cover the base with paper strips. Fasten the wide end of the base to the wide end of the ball with more strips. Cover the hole with strips. Let the ball dry.

5 Draw a basket shape on the ball. Draw the handle. Cut out the shape. Spray-paint the basket white. When completely dry, apply tissue paper (see tip *at right*).

COLORFUL COVERAGE Paint small areas of the basket with the gloss medium and varnish. Lay cut strips of tissue paper over the medium. Paint the medium over the top of the tissue paper. Cover all sides of the basket with the tissue paper. Let dry.

PAPER BOWLS Make bowls just like the baskets, except do not cut handles. Cut or tear different colors of tissue paper and fasten these to the bowl sides with the gloss medium and varnish to make designs. The insides of our bowls use just one color of paper. Add a contrasting color of tissue paper around the rim of the bowl.

PUMPKIN MASK This pumpkin mask is built up over an extra-large balloon with layers of paper-mache and covered with layers of orange tissue paper. Cut out the base so the mask fits over your head. Mark the eyes, nose, and mouth placements and cut out and trim them with black paper. Cut cardboard leaves and cover them with green tissue paper. Wrap paper twist with green paper for the vine.

BIRD PIÑATA Two balloons, one for the body and one for the head, are the beginnings of this colorful bird. His wings and tail are made of poster board and his legs are pieces of dowels. Trim the bird with bright feathers and use construction paper to make his eyes and beak. To use him as a piñata, cut out a circle in the back of the bird body and fill the inside with candies. Reglue the circle in place.

THE LAST STRAW

Here, bundles of drinking straws form interesting sculptures. Shape them, paint them, and trim them with party favors to make a centerpiece decoration to celebrate the Fourth of July or Valentine's Day.

1 Thread the needle with a double strand of thread that measures about 20 inches long. Knot the end, leaving a 4-inch tail.

3 Tie the beginning and end tail threads into a knot to form a bundle of straws that is drawn together in the middle.

2 Working on a flat surface, sew 18 to 25 straws together in a row. Alternate the placement of the straws as shown in the photo, *above*. Cut the thread, leaving a 4-inch tail.

4 Twist and bend the straws to form an interesting shape.

5 Spray-paint the sculpture and add party trims to decorate it.

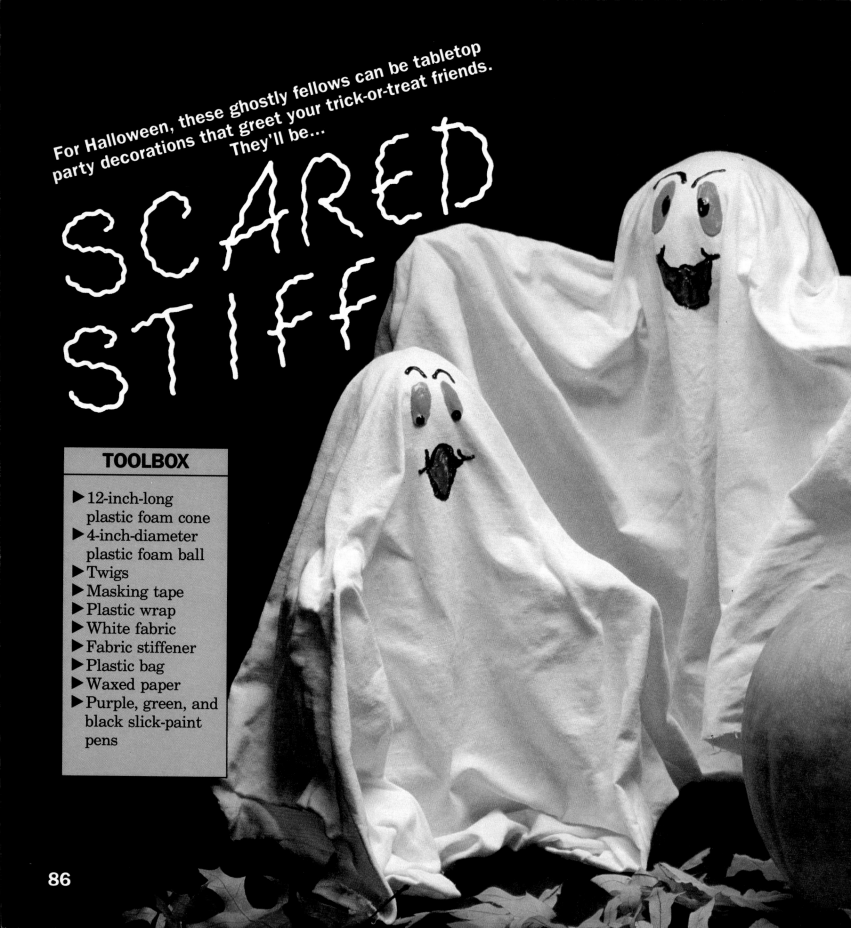

For Halloween, these ghostly fellows can be tabletop party decorations that greet your trick-or-treat friends. They'll be...

SCARED STIFF

TOOLBOX

► 12-inch-long plastic foam cone
► 4-inch-diameter plastic foam ball
► Twigs
► Masking tape
► Plastic wrap
► White fabric
► Fabric stiffener
► Plastic bag
► Waxed paper
► Purple, green, and black slick-paint pens

1 Referring to the drawing *at left,* assemble the form for the ghost. Insert a short straight twig into the ball and the top of the cone. Use masking tape to fasten the twigs together to make arms. Insert twig arms into the sides of the cone. Cover the entire shape with plastic wrap.

2 Cut a piece of white fabric into a square or circle that will fully cover the form with some extra for draping.

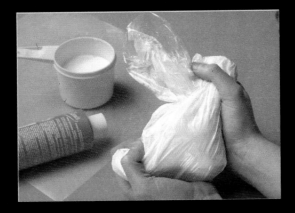

3 Pour 1 cup of fabric stiffener into the plastic bag. Place the fabric piece in the bag. Squeeze the bag repeatedly to soak the fabric with stiffener. Add more stiffener to the bag, if necessary.

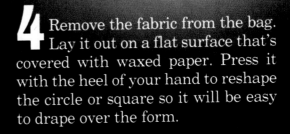

4 Remove the fabric from the bag. Lay it out on a flat surface that's covered with waxed paper. Press it with the heel of your hand to reshape the circle or square so it will be easy to drape over the form.

5 Place the fabric over the form and drape it to shape a ghost. Keep some of the fabric along the base so the ghost will stand by itself when it's removed from the form. Let the fabric dry.

Paint on eyes, eyebrows, and a mouth. Remove the ghost from the form. Use the form again to make another ghost.

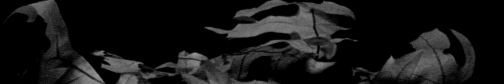

Bubble Teasers

What fun to blow and wave bubbles from these cookie-cutter bubble wands! No matter what shape, the bubbles still come out like a sphere. There're great to make and give as party favors.

TOOLBOX

- ▶ Cookie cutters
- ▶ Bell wire (available at lumberyards or home center stores)
- ▶ Cinnamon sticks
- ▶ Scissors

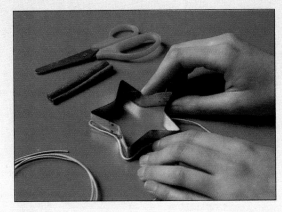

1 Beginning at the center bottom of the cookie cutter, and leaving a wire tail of about 1½ inches, shape the wire around the outside edges.

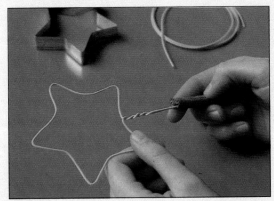

2 Cut the wire, leaving a second 1½-inch tail. Twist the tail ends together. Insert the twisted ends into a hole in a cinnamon stick.

Because these wands are bigger than those that come with the purchased bubble liquid, pour the liquid into a pie tin or cereal-size bowl.

BUBBLE LIQUID
Use purchased bubble liquid or make your own by mixing liquid detergent with a little bit of water. If you want colored bubbles, add a few drops of food coloring to the mixture.

Flies Time

A painted birdhouse turns into a clock. Build one for yourself and you'll see that...

3 Paint the house, door, and chimes. Let the paint dry.

4 Remove the hands from the clockwork. Spread glue around the outside edges of the clockwork. Working from inside the house, center the clockwork stem in the circle opening and fasten the clockwork in place. Reattach the hands. Trim the hands with scissors.

5 Place the door against the house and mark the positions for the hinges. The sanded edge of the door is the hinged side. Glue, then nail the hinges to the door. For a knob on the door, center the ½-inch nail on the opposite side of the door and hammer in place. Place the door back in position on the house and nail the hinges to the ends of the house.

6 Screw the hooks into the bottom of the house, placing them 1 inch apart and 1 inch from the front edge. Slip dowels onto these hooks. Fasten adhesive numbers to the front of the house. Attach the picture hanger to the back of house at the roof peak.

1 If you are using a purchased birdhouse, carefully remove one side of the house. If you bought a kit, assemble it following the manufacturer's instructions, *except* do not attach one of the sides to the house. This side will be hinged to the house as a door, making it easy to fasten the clockwork and to change the batteries. Sand off about ⅛ inch along one side of the door.

2 Cut the dowel into one 11-inch piece and one 13-inch piece for the chimes. Screw the eye screws into one end of each dowel.

TOOLBOX

- Purchased assembled birdhouse or birdhouse kit
- Sandpaper
- ⅝-inch-diameter dowel, 24 inches long
- Two small eye screws and hooks
- Acrylic paints
- Foam brushes
- Narrow paint-brush
- Battery-operated clockwork with 1-inch stem
- Extra-tacky glue
- Pair of small hinges
- ¾-inch plastic adhesive numbers
- ½-inch flathead nail
- Picture hanger
- Transparent tape

PAINTING STRIPES Use transparent tape to define stripe areas on the dowels and clock face. Paint the stripe, then pull away the tape. Repeat again to make another stripe.

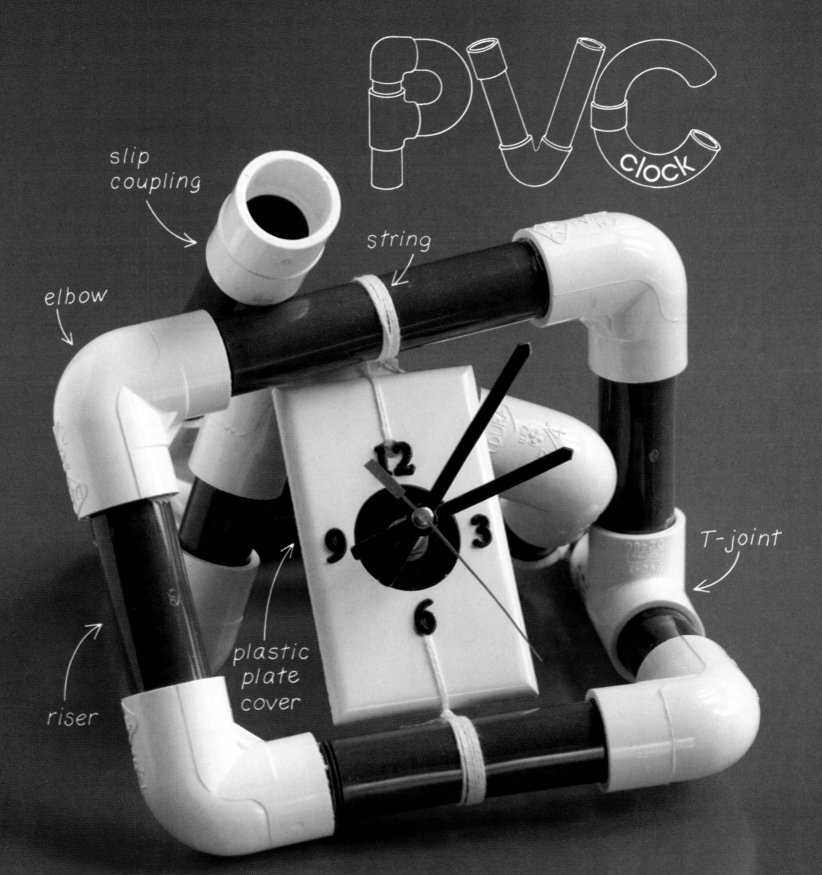

PVC clock

slip coupling

string

elbow

T-joint

riser

plastic plate cover

12
9
3
6

Design your own clock that's guaranteed to create lots of conversation. Its frame is made from PVC pipe and plastic paraphernalia that can be bought at home supply centers.

TOOLBOX

▶ 15- or 20-amp single receptacle plastic plate cover
▶ 90-degree ¾-inch PVC T-joint
▶ 90-degree ¾-inch PVC elbows
▶ ¾-inch diameter risers ranging in size from 3 to 6 inches
▶ Two 60-inch-long pieces of white string
▶ Battery operated clockwork with 1-inch stem
▶ ½-inch plastic adhesive numbers
▶ White crafts glue suitable for plastics

CUT YOUR OWN

You can buy ¾-inch-diameter PVC tubing and cut it into shorter lengths instead of using risers. It's a lot cheaper. First, ask your parents if you can use their handsaw to cut the pieces.

1 Join elbows and T-joints with risers to create an interesting shape. Keep in mind that you will want to have two risers about 4½ inches apart on which to fasten the plate cover that holds the clockwork. When you like the shape, glue the pieces together. Let the glue dry.

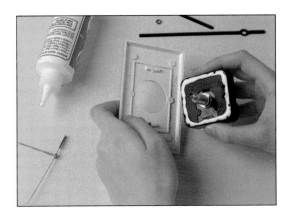

2 Remove the hands from the clockwork. Centering the stem through the hole, glue the clockwork to the back side of the plate cover.

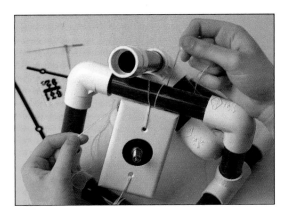

3 Threading the string through the screw holes in the plate, position and wrap the ends of the string around the risers. Knot the ends of the string. Add a dot of glue to the knot and trim the ends.

4 Apply adhesive numbers to the front of the plate. Reattach the hands to the stem of the clockwork.

buttons, bangles, & beads

You can make beads, buttons, earrings, pins, and pendants.

1 From each color of the modeling compound, cut a small wedge and roll it into a ball. Knead the ball until it's soft and pliable. Roll the ball into spaghetti-like strands.

3 Squeeze the strand together on the knitting needle and roll it back and forth on a flat surface as you would a rolling pin.

2 Twist two or three different color strands together. Roll this strand until it is smooth and even. Wrap the strand around the knitting needle.

4 Use the knife to cut the strand into beads. Slide the beads off the knitting needle. Place them on the cookie sheet. Continue to make more beads following these instructions. Bake the beads in an oven as directed on the modeling compound package. When the beads are cool, string the beads to make a necklace, bracelet, or other pieces of jewelery.

MODELING COMPOUND Cernit or Fimo plasticlike modeling compound can be purchased at crafts or art supply stores. It comes in small packages and lots of colors. You'll find it's easy to work with and can be shaped into lots of designs—you'll discover many uses for this material as you play with it.

We used a toothpick to make holes for buttons before baking them in the oven. For checkerboards, we cut flat, narrow strips and wove them over and under. For swirling designs, we layered flattened rectangles and rolled the layers into a tube, then cut the tube into narrow slices.

Tree Treats

These ice-cream cones look good enough to eat! They're so easy to make, you'll want to make them by the dozens as gifts for teachers and friends.

TOOLBOX

- ▶ Box of sugar cones
- ▶ 2-inch-diameter plastic foam balls
- ▶ Jar of acrylic gloss medium and varnish
- ▶ Jar of modeling paste
- ▶ Crafts glue
- ▶ Paintbrush
- ▶ Knife or spreader
- ▶ Staples or tops of cut-off paper clips
- ▶ Waxed paper
- ▶ Poster or acrylic paints
- ▶ Shoe box

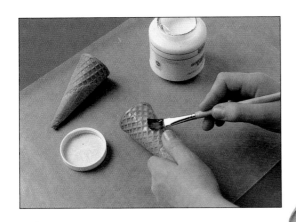

1 Cover your work area with a sheet of waxed paper. Paint the inside and outside of the ice-cream cone with the gloss varnish. Set the cone aside to dry on waxed paper for at least 24 hours.

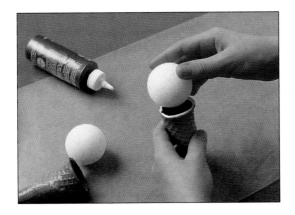

2 Squeeze a band of crafts glue around the inside rim of the cone. Set a ball on top of the cone and push the ball into the glue.

3 Dab glue on the tips of a staple or paper clip and push the tips into the top of the ball. Set the ornament aside to let the glue dry.

4 Cut 1-inch-diameter holes in the lid of a shoe box. Use the knife to spread the modeling paste over the ball, taking care not to cover the staple or paper clip. Set the cone in the lid of the box to allow the modeling paste to dry.

5 Using poster or acrylic paint, paint the ice cream the color of your favorite flavor.

Even if there's no snow on the ground, you can make this trio of snowmen. The how-to steps show you how to make the snow lady. But the steps are the same for all of them.

FROSTY FOLKS FROSTYFRO

TOOLBOX

- 1-pound package of gray instant paper-mache
- Mixing bowl
- 4- and 3½-inch-diameter plastic foam balls for small snowmen
- 4-, 3½-, and 3-inch-diameter balls for large snowman
- 4-inch-diameter plastic foam ring for lady's hat
- Toothpick
- Crafts glue
- White, orange, and red acrylic paints
- Glue-on doll eyes
- Whole cloves
- Assorted buttons
- Felt for scarfs
- ¼-inch-wide ribbon for hat ties
- Black construction paper and a sock for hats
- Twigs for arms
- Dried flowers for lady's hat trim
- Two foam brushes
- Small paintbrush

1 In the mixing bowl, mix about one-fourth of the instant paper-mache with ¾ cup of warm water. Cover and place it in the refrigerator for about 2 hours. When ready to begin, knead the paper-mache clay on a flat surface until it is soft and at room temperature. *Note:* As you work, cover the clay that you are not using with plastic wrap.

2 To make the snow lady, use the 3- and 4-inch-diameter balls. Flatten two *opposite* sides of the larger ball and one side of the smaller ball by pounding them on a hard surface. Squeeze glue onto one of the flat sides of the larger ball. Insert a toothpick in the center of the flat side. Fasten the smaller ball on top for the head.

3 To apply the paper-mache clay, firmly press a small amount (about the size of a small marble) onto one ball. Dip your fingers into a bowl with warm water. Rub your wet fingers over the clay to smooth the surface. Continue to add the clay in this manner until the balls are covered.

4 Use a rolling pin to roll over the ring to flatten the curved edges. Cover the ring with clay. Then place the ring on top of the head. Fill in the gap between the ring and the head to blend the two pieces together.

TURN THE PAGE ▶

FOR THE LADY'S HAT

To finish the snow lady's hat, glue ribbons along the sides of the face. Tie another piece of ribbon into a bow. Glue the bow under the chin. Glue dried flowers along the hat's brim.

FOR THE SOCK HAT

Referring to the drawing *below*, make an overhand knot in a sock slightly above the heel. Pull the knot tightly. Measure about 4 inches from the knot along the foot portion of the sock. Cut off the remaining foot and toe portions. Cut several ½-inch-wide slits up to the knot to make a fringed tassel. Pull the ribbed end of the sock over the head of the snowman. Fold back the ribbing twice.

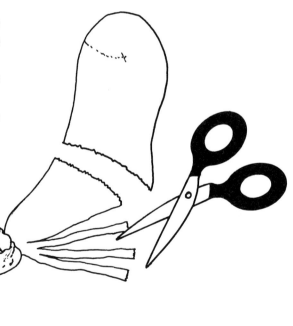

5 For the carrot nose, use your hands to roll a small piece of clay into the shape of a carrot. Insert a toothpick into the center of the face. Push the carrot nose over the toothpick and slide it up against the face.

6 Position and push the eyes and buttons into the clay. Push the twig arms and whole cloves for the mouth into the clay and into the foam ball. Remove all these parts from the snowman once they have made indentations. These items will be glued in place in Step 9. Set the snowman aside for at least 2 to 3 days to let the clay completely dry.

7 Mix 4 tablespoons of glue with 2 tablespoons of water. Use a foam brush to apply the mixture to the snowman. Let the glue mixture dry for about 20 to 30 minutes.

8 Use another foam brush to paint the snowman white. Use the small brush to paint the carrot nose orange. Paint the hat red. Let the paint dry.

9 Glue the eyes, cloves, twig arms, and buttons in the same places where you made the indentations in Step 6.

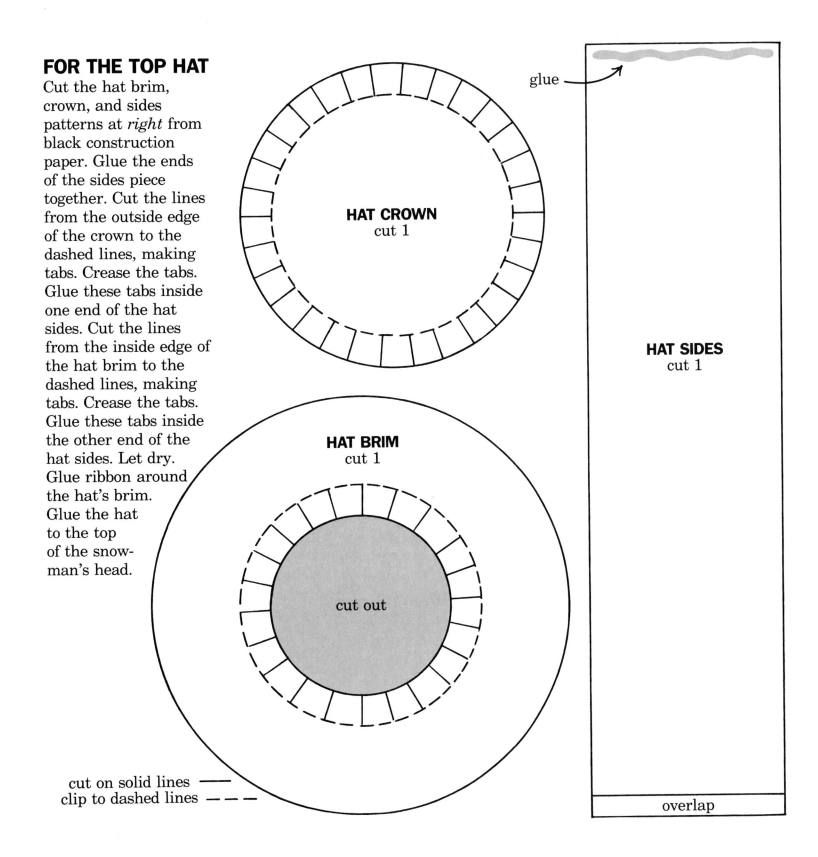

FOR THE TOP HAT

Cut the hat brim, crown, and sides patterns at *right* from black construction paper. Glue the ends of the sides piece together. Cut the lines from the outside edge of the crown to the dashed lines, making tabs. Crease the tabs. Glue these tabs inside one end of the hat sides. Cut the lines from the inside edge of the hat brim to the dashed lines, making tabs. Crease the tabs. Glue these tabs inside the other end of the hat sides. Let dry. Glue ribbon around the hat's brim. Glue the hat to the top of the snowman's head.

HAT CROWN
cut 1

glue

HAT SIDES
cut 1

HAT BRIM
cut 1

cut out

cut on solid lines ———
clip to dashed lines – – –

overlap

THE GREATEST
DOUGH ON EARTH

Use flour, salt, and water to knead a dough. Then follow the instructions to make the elephant. Or, create any of the other animals here or the objects on the following two pages.

TOOLBOX

▶ 2 cups flour
▶ 1 cup salt
▶ 1 cup hot water
▶ Mixing bowl
▶ Mixing spoon
▶ Cookie sheet
▶ Cutting board
▶ Toothpicks
▶ Scissors
▶ Paintbrush
▶ Acrylic paints

1 Mix the flour and salt together in the mixing bowl. Gradually add the hot water to the flour and salt, stirring with the spoon. Lift the dough from the bowl and knead it on a flat surface for about 10 minutes.

2 For the elephant, shape a large ball of dough for the body. Shape a smaller ball for the head. Place the balls on the cookie sheet and bake them in a 200° oven for 2½ hours. Remove them from the oven and let cool.

3 Roll a tube of dough about ¼ inch in diameter. From this tube, cut a tail about 1½ inches long. Use extra dough to secure the tail to the body. Use warm water on your fingertips to smooth the extra dough on the ball.

4 Roll a tube of dough about ½ inch in diameter. From this tube, cut four 1-inch pieces for the legs. Push toothpicks into the ends of each leg. Insert the toothpicks into the body and slide the legs up to fit against the body. Cut off the toothpick ends. Use extra dough to fill in the gaps between the body and legs. Smooth the edges.

5 Join the head to the body using extra dough. Bake this unit in the oven for about 1 hour.

6 Make two thin ovals for ears and fasten them to the sides of the head. Roll a tapered tube to make the trunk. Fasten it to the front of the head. Add smaller tapered strands to the sides of the trunk for the tusks.

7 Bake the elephant in the oven for 2 hours. Let cool. Paint the elephant in colors of your choice.

105

MORE DOUGH PROJECTS

For the train, form just the box-shaped cars and bake them in the oven for about 1½ hours. Then make the wheels. Use toothpicks to fasten the wheels to the cars. Return the cars with the wheels to the oven and bake them for another 2 hours. Have lots of fun painting them. You might glue a ½-inch-wide strip of felt to the bottom of the cars to join them together.

MR. PANDA

Shape a panda bear by making a larger dough ball for the body and a smaller ball for the head. Bake the balls in the oven for about 1½ hours. Join the head and body together with extra dough. Add tubular arms, legs, and oval-shaped ears. Bake the assembled bear for another 2 hours. Paint the panda black and white.

CHUNKY-CHOO

TABLE FOR 2

Make dollhouse furniture from extra dough. Shape tables and chairs from flat rectangles of dough. Use toothpicks to secure the legs. Turn the pieces upside down to bake in the oven. Once you've got the technique down, you can make a stove, refrigerator, dishes, bed, and lots more furniture and dollhouse accessories.

YOUR OWN DOUGH ART

When you begin to construct an item, think about all the different shapes that make up the whole piece—a cube, rectangle, sphere, or tube. Mold each of the parts separately. First bake the larger pieces. Then assemble the whole object, using extra dough to hold the large and small pieces together.

107

STASH THE CASH

Stow your earned money in a cork cottage bank to save up for a bike, baseball bat, ice skates, cassette, or other item on your wish list.

TOOLBOX

▶ Roll of ⅛- or ¹⁄₁₆-inch-thick cork
▶ Tracing paper
▶ No. 2 pencil
▶ Felt-tip pen
▶ Two ½-gallon empty milk cartons for the base of the bank
▶ Cork stopper
▶ Manicure scissors and regular scissors
▶ Crafts glue
▶ Pink, white, and green slick-paint pens
▶ Jars of red, yellow, and blue acrylic paints
▶ Paintbrush

1 Trace the cottage patterns on pages 111 and 112 onto tracing paper. With the No. 2 pencil, color over the traced lines on the *back* side of the tracing paper. If you want to draw your own doors, windows, and other designs on the cottage, trace only the outlines of the patterns.

3 Position the cork cottage pieces along the bottom edges of one of the milk cartons. Draw the top lines of the shapes onto the carton using the felt-tip marker. Cut out the cottage base from the carton.

2 With the colored side of the tracing paper facing the cork, trace the cottage patterns onto the cork. Draw your designs on the sides and roof pieces of the cottage if you chose to draw your own. After all the tracing or drawing is complete, cut out the shapes from the cork.

4 For the roof, lay a cork roof piece on one side of the second milk carton and draw around the shape. Line up and draw the roof on a side of the carton that borders the first side. Cut out the roof, leaving the pieces attached at the corner crease. In the center of the crease, cut a 1-inch-long slit for the money slot. (See the slit in the photo for Step 5 on the next page.)

TURN THE PAGE ▶

5 Position the cork stopper in the center of one of the milk carton roof sides and draw around the shape. Use the manicure scissors to cut out the circle, cutting slightly beyond the drawn line so about one-third of the cork fits into the hole.

7 First glue the cork sides to *opposite* sides of the milk carton base. Then glue the front and back cork pieces to the base. Trim the ends of the sides, if necessary, to fit.

6 Lay one of the cork roof pieces under the carton roof and draw around the circle. Make sure the cork piece lies so the untraced side faces the milk carton and the shingle pattern goes in the right direction. Cut out the cork circle. Glue the cork roof pieces to the carton roof.

8 Paint the cottage following the drawn lines on the cork and using the colors in the photo on page 108 as a guide. Use the white slick paint to fill in the spaces at the peak of the roof and the side corners of the house. Do not fill in the money slot you cut in the roof.

CORK ORNAMENTS

Use the leftover cork to make cookie-cutter ornaments like the ones on page 111. Lay cookie cutters on top of the cork and draw around the shapes. Cut out ornaments on the drawn lines. Use a hole punch to make holes in the tops of the ornaments to thread ribbon or cording. Decorate the ornaments with acrylic or slick-pen paints. Then thread ribbon or cording through the holes for hanging. Knot the ends to make a loop.

CORK TIP The rolled cork may not lie flat when you unroll it. Before beginning to work with the cork, lay it on a flat surface and cover it with a damp towel. Cover the towel with waxed paper or aluminum foil and put books or other heavy objects on the paper or foil. Let it sit overnight.

BANK ROOF
cut 2

BANK SIDE
cut 2

BANK FRONT
cut 1

BANK BACK
cut 1

112

PLAYFUL
PUPPETS

Merry Lionette

Marionettes are puppets with jointed arms and legs that are moved by pulling on strings attached to a frame. Once you've made this sunny-faced lion, you can create lots more characters and cast a show.

TOOLBOX

- ▶ Four cardboard tissue tubes
- ▶ Yellow and orange gloss spray paint
- ▶ Two sheets of 11x14-inch poster board
- ▶ Tracing paper
- ▶ Black slick-paint pen
- ▶ Hammer and nail
- ▶ Old wooden board
- ▶ Six ½-inch-diameter buttons
- ▶ 2 yards of clothesline rope cut to the following lengths: one 9 inches (neck), one 10 inches (tail), and two 22 inches (legs)
- ▶ Carpet thread cut into six 36-inch-long strands
- ▶ Sewing needle
- ▶ Paper punch
- ▶ Three paint stirring sticks
- ▶ Tacky glue

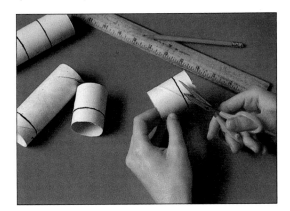

1 Draw rings that measure 1½ inches long around both ends of two tissue tubes for the four foot spacers. Draw one ring that measures ¾ inch long around one end of one tube for the neck spacer. To cut out the spacers, cut through the center of the tube. Then cut down to the drawn rings and cut out the pieces. Use one whole tube for the body.

2 Spray both sides of one piece of poster board yellow. Spray both sides of the other piece orange. Spray the four feet and neck spacers yellow. Spray the body tube orange. Let the paint dry.

3 Trace the patterns on pages 118 and 119 onto tracing paper and cut them out. Trace the patterns onto the painted poster boards and cut them out. Use the black slick pen to draw a face onto the face piece using the pattern as a guide.

TURN THE PAGE ▶

115

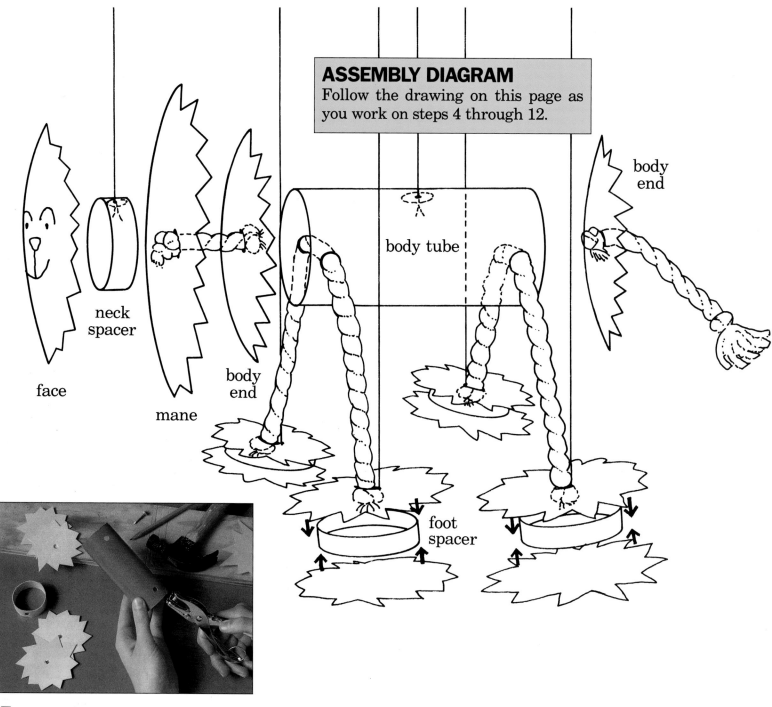

body end

body tube

neck spacer

face

mane

body end

foot spacer

4 Working over the wooden board, use the hammer and nail to punch holes in the center of the mane, the body end pieces, and just four of the foot pieces. Push the tip of a pencil through the holes to make them larger.

Use the paper punch to make one hole in the center of the neck spacer.

Use the needle to punch one hole in the center of the body tube. Use the paper punch to punch four holes in the tube, about ½ inch from the ends, for the rope legs.

116

5 Center and glue the four *punched* foot pieces to one side of each of the four foot spacers.

Center and glue the neck spacer to one side of the mane.

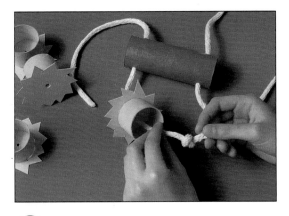

6 Thread the two 22-inch-long rope pieces through the leg holes in the body. Push each of the rope ends through the holes of the four feet pieces. Tie overhand knots at the ends of each rope.

7 Tie a button at the end of one length of carpet thread. Push the other end through the hole of the neck spacer, pulling the thread through until the button rests against the hole.

8 Make an overhand knot in one end of the 9-inch-long rope. Thread the rope through the mane and into one of the body end pieces. Make an overhand knot in the end of the rope, leaving about a 2-inch gap of rope for the neck between the mane and body piece. Glue the face to the other end of the neck spacer. Make sure the hole in the spacer is on the top side. Glue the body end piece to the body tube. Make sure the hole in the body tube is on the top side.

TURN THE PAGE ▶

MORE ANIMAL MARIONETTES

Following the steps for the lion, you can use tubes, small boxes, egg cartons, or assemble triangular cardboard wedges to create more animal puppets like those shown *below*.

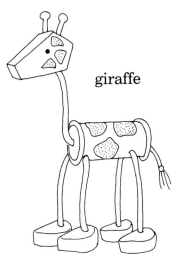

giraffe

zebra

crocodile

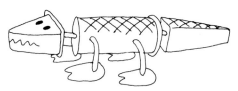

9 Thread the needle with one of the 36-inch-long carpet threads. Push the needle through the hole at the top of the body. Reach into the tube and pull it out through the open end of the tube. Remove the needle from the thread. Tie a button to the end of the thread. Pull gently on the thread until the button rests against the hole in the inside of the tube.

10 For the tail, make an over-hand knot in one end of the 10-inch-long rope piece. Thread the other end through the remaining body end piece. Glue the body end piece to the end of the body.

Tie an overhand knot about 1 inch from the end of the rope and split the fibers to fringe the tail.

11 Tie a button to each of the four remaining lengths of thread. Push each thread through the holes of each of the foot pieces so the buttons rest next to the knots. Center and glue the foot spacers to the remaining four foot pieces.

12 For the wooden frame, glue two paint stirring sticks about 3 inches apart on top of the third stick as shown in the diagram *at right*. Let glue dry.

13 Following the same diagram, wrap and tie the six 36-inch-long carpet threads around the paint sticks. Adjust the threads to make sure the puppet stands straight. Dab glue onto the knots to hold them in place.

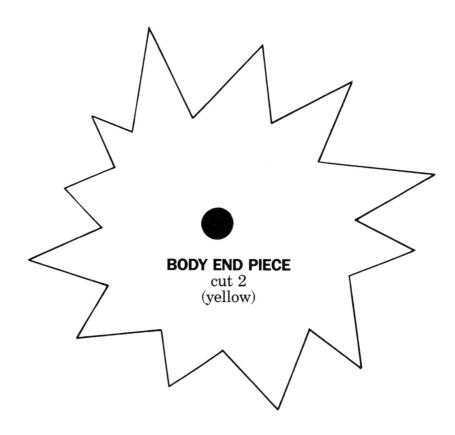

left back leg

left front leg

body

head

right back leg

right front leg

PUPPET FRAME

BODY END PIECE
cut 2
(yellow)

MANE
cut 1
(orange)

FACE
cut 1
(yellow)

FOOT PIECE
cut 8
(yellow)

119

CATCH OF THE DAY

Mr. Walrus and his fishy friends are sea creatures made of felt. No sewing needed–just cut and glue these perky puppets.

TOOLBOX

- 9x12-inch pieces of gray felt and white felt
- Scraps of black, red, and orange felt for the walrus
- Assorted scraps of felt for the fish
- Six rubber bands
- Extra-tacky glue
- Tracing paper
- Straight pins
- Large-eye sewing needle; toothpick
- 1-inch length of no-sew self-grip fastening tape

1 Trace the walrus and fish patterns on pages 122 and 123 onto tracing paper. Cut out the patterns.

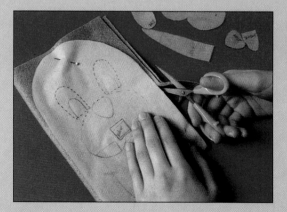

2 Fold the gray felt square in half and pin the walrus head pattern on top. Cutting through both layers of felt, cut out two head pieces.

3 Cut out the eyes, nose, muzzle, tusks, tongue, and fish patterns from felt. Cut the fish from felt colors of your choice. Use a pencil to mark the dots on the felt muzzle for placements of the whiskers.

4 Glue the pupils on top of the eyes. Glue the eyes to one of the head pieces.

TURN THE PAGE ▶

PUPPET TIP

Extra-tacky glue will hold your puppet pieces together. Make sure the glue is completely dry before you place the puppet over your hand and have fun with it.

NOSE
cut 1
(black)

TUSK
cut 2
(white)

5 Cut the rubber bands and make an overhand knot in one end of each one. Thread the needle with a rubber band. Pull the needle up through one of the dots on the muzzle until the knot rests against the back side of the muzzle. Remove the needle. Sew the remaining rubber bands to the muzzle.

6 Use the toothpick to spread glue on the back of the muzzle (above the blue line marked on the pattern). Fasten the muzzle to the head.

7 Glue the black nose to the muzzle. Lift the muzzle and glue the tongue to the head. Spread glue on the tusks (above the blue line marked on the pattern) and glue them to the head. Place the tops of the tusks under the muzzle.

8 Glue the eye pieces and the fin to the fish. Pull the strip of self-grip fastening tape apart so there are two pieces. Glue one piece to the wrong side of the fish, as shown on the pattern. Lift the muzzle and glue the other piece above the mouth.

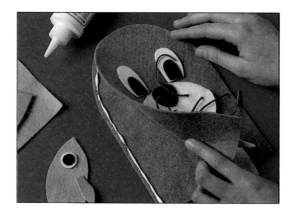

9 Squeeze a band of glue around all edges of the other head piece, *except the bottom edge.* Carefully matching the edges, glue the two head pieces together. Let dry. Matching the strips of fastening tape, attach the fish in the walrus's mouth.

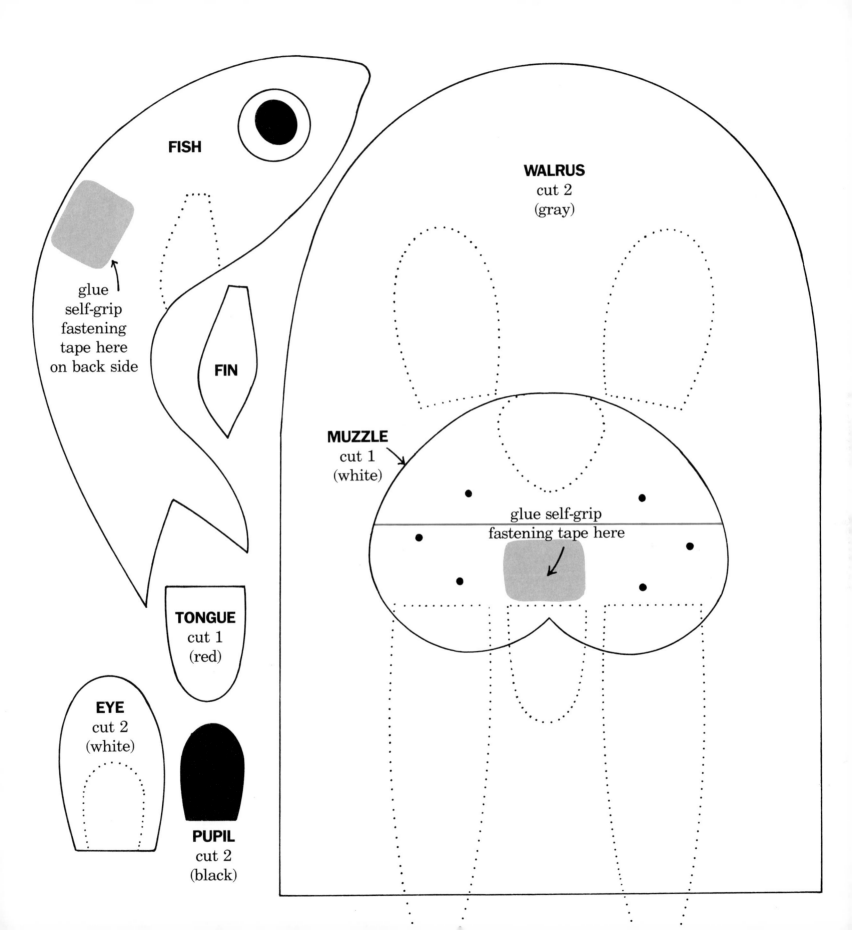

FISH

glue
self-grip
fastening
tape here
on back side

FIN

WALRUS
cut 2
(gray)

MUZZLE
cut 1
(white)

glue self-grip
fastening tape here

TONGUE
cut 1
(red)

EYE
cut 2
(white)

PUPIL
cut 2
(black)

CEREAL

BOX
CRITTERS

A one-serving-size cereal box provides the base for our three silly hand puppets. Make a zany bird, a crazy creature, or a lovable lion.

1 Carefully open one end of the cereal box. Remove the lining bag with the cereal. Glue closed the end that you opened.

2 Working over newspapers in a well-ventilated area, spray all sides of the box with several coats of red paint.

3 Refer to the Step 3 diagram at *right*. On the side of the cereal box without the perforation marks, cut the box in half, cutting through the top and down both of the narrow sides. The dashed lines show the cutting lines. Do not cut through the bottom side.

4 Refer to the Step 4 diagram at *right*. Fold the box in half against itself. The inside of the box becomes the place where you put your fingers so you can open and close the box like a mouth.

5 Trace the patterns for the creature puppet on pages 126 and 127 onto tracing paper. Cut out the patterns. Cut out the patterns from the colored papers as listed on the patterns. Cut the slits in the stars.

TURN THE PAGE ▶

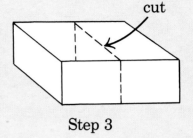

cut

Step 3

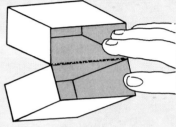

Step 4

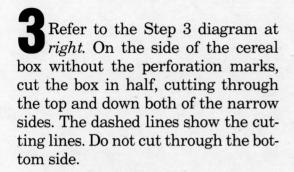

TOP LIP
cut 1
(gold)

BOTTOM LIP
cut 1
(gold)

PUPPET FUN You can create lots of puppets using this same cereal box technique. Save those small cereal boxes and prepare them by following steps 1–4 of the instructions on pages 124 and 125. Instructions for the bird and lion puppets are on the next four pages. Or you can design your own creatures using paper scraps, yarns, stickers, feathers, and other interesting materials. You might even want to make a stage for your puppets, write a play, or just gather your friends together for an afternoon of puppet chatter.

6 Use the black marker to outline the lips. Glue the top lip to the end of the top half of the box. Glue the bottom lip to the end of the bottom half of the box. Accordion-pleat the end of the tongue using the dashed lines on the pattern as a guide. Glue the tongue to the top of the bottom half of the box.

7 Glue the table tennis balls on top of the top half of the box for eyes. Use a paper punch to make light blue pupils and glue them to the center front of the table tennis balls.

EYELASHES
cut 2
(black)

slit
slit

ANTENNAE STARS
cut 2
(red)

TONGUE
cut 1
(green)

pleat pleat pleat pleat

poke holes here

Step 9

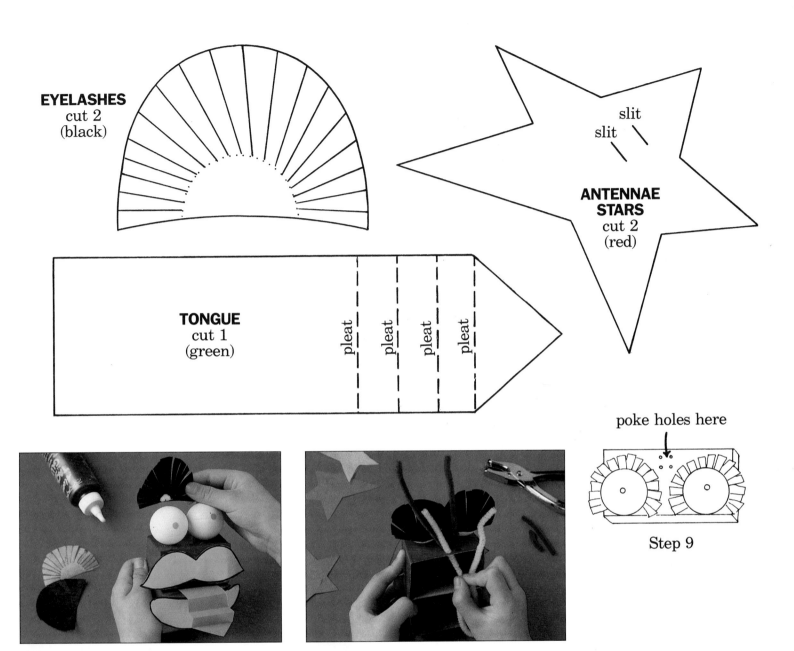

8 Fringe the eyelashes by cutting on the lines. Glue an eyelash behind each eye.

9 Use the point of the pencil to poke four holes in the center of the top half of the box (see the diagram, *right*).

10 Fold the two pipe cleaners in half. From the underside of the top half of the box, push one end through each hole. Place the stars on the ends of the front pipe cleaners. Bend the other two ends into zigzags.

FOR THE LION PUPPET

1 Follow steps 1–4 on pages 124 and 125 to prepare the cereal box. We painted the box black.

2 For the head piece, use a glue stick to glue two 9x12-inch sheets of different color paper together. Trace the head piece pattern onto tracing paper. Fold the glued paper in half. Place the fold of the pattern on the fold of the paper and cut out one head piece.

3 Referring to the drawing at *right,* glue the tab to the underside of the top box. Glue the fangs to the wrong side of the face following the placement line on the pattern. Bring the face to the front of the top box and glue it in place.

4 For the nose, trace the nose pattern onto tracing paper. Cut out one yellow nose.

5 Fold back the tabs along the sides of the nose. Following the placement lines on the head pattern, glue the nose tabs to the front of the face (head piece).

6 Cut out two large eyes from white paper and two smaller eyes from colored paper. Glue the colored eyes to the white eyes. Following the placement line for the eyes on the head piece, glue the eyes to the face. Use a paper punch to make two black pupils and glue them to the eyes.

Step 3
Glue tab inside box top

7 Cut six narrow strips of black paper about 5 inches long for the whiskers. Curl one end of each strip around a pencil. Glue three uncurled ends to each side of the face.

PAPER TIP We glued contrasting colors of paper together for more interesting and colorful effects. Notice how the lion head has a blue side and a yellow side. This doubled thickness of paper also makes the head piece stronger. Use a glue stick to fasten the sheets together before cutting out the pattern pieces.

128

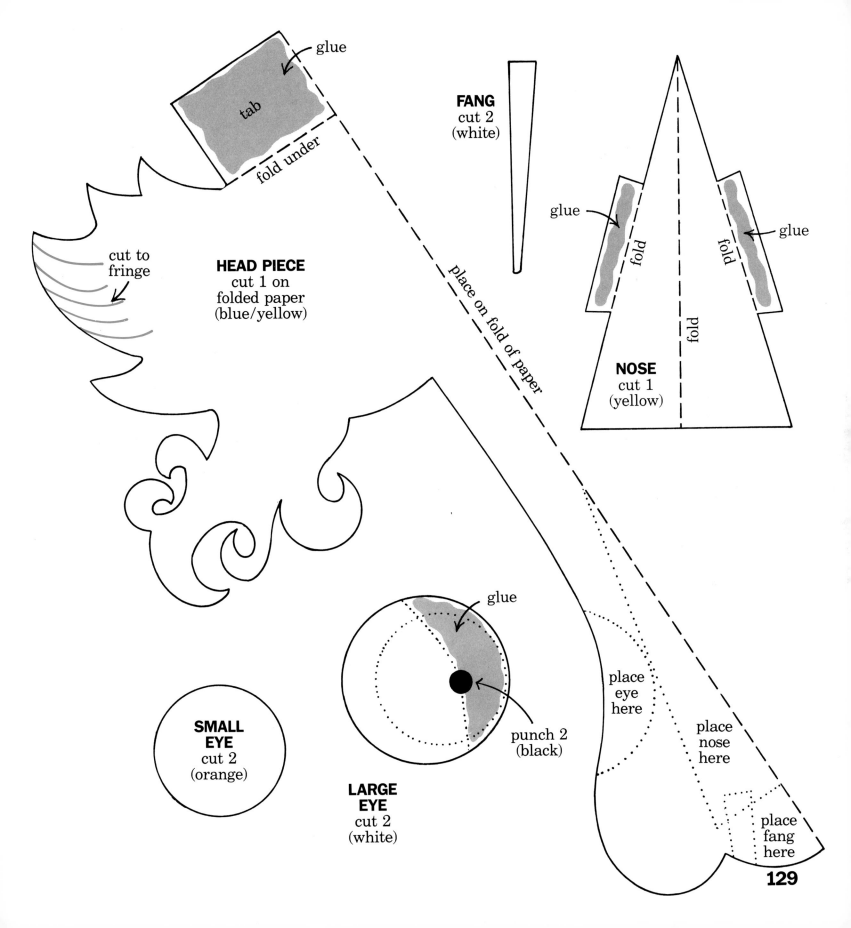

glue

tab

fold under

FANG
cut 2
(white)

glue

fold

fold

glue

fold

NOSE
cut 1
(yellow)

cut to
fringe

HEAD PIECE
cut 1 on
folded paper
(blue/yellow)

place on fold of paper

glue

punch 2
(black)

SMALL
EYE
cut 2
(orange)

LARGE
EYE
cut 2
(white)

place
eye
here

place
nose
here

place
fang
here

129

FOR THE BIRD PUPPET

1 Follow steps 1–4 on pages 124 and 125 to prepare the cereal box. We painted the box blue.

2 For the head piece, use a glue stick to glue two 9x12-inch sheets of orange paper together (see Paper Tip on page 128). Trace the head piece pattern onto tracing paper. Fold the orange paper in half. Place the fold of the pattern on the fold of the orange paper and cut out one head piece.

3 Referring to the drawing at *right,* glue the flaps at the "A" ends of the head piece to the front end of the top box. Glue the center of the face to the same box end. Fold *up* the tab in the center of the face (do not glue it).

4 For the beak, fold a yellow sheet of paper in half and glue the halves together. Trace the beak pattern onto tracing paper. Cut out two yellow beaks.

5 Crease the beaks along the fold lines marked on the pattern. With the crease facing out, and referring to the drawing at *right,* glue the shaded portion of one beak to the *top* of the bottom box, inside the mouth. In the same way, glue the second beak to the *bottom* of the top box.

Step 3

Step 5

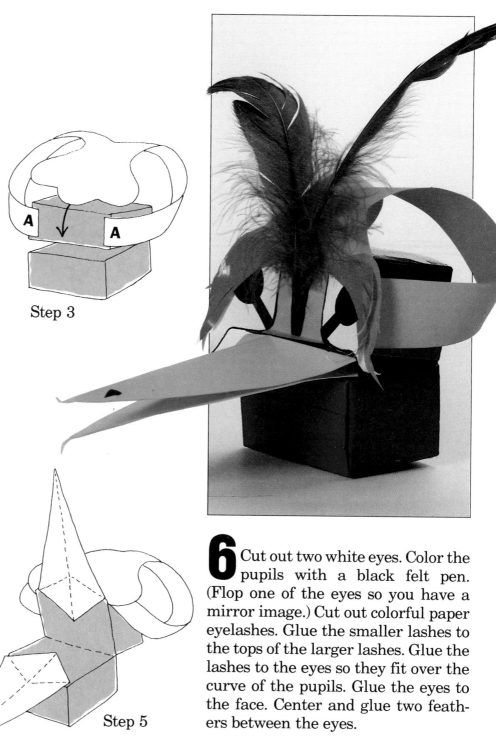

6 Cut out two white eyes. Color the pupils with a black felt pen. (Flop one of the eyes so you have a mirror image.) Cut out colorful paper eyelashes. Glue the smaller lashes to the tops of the larger lashes. Glue the lashes to the eyes so they fit over the curve of the pupils. Glue the eyes to the face. Center and glue two feathers between the eyes.

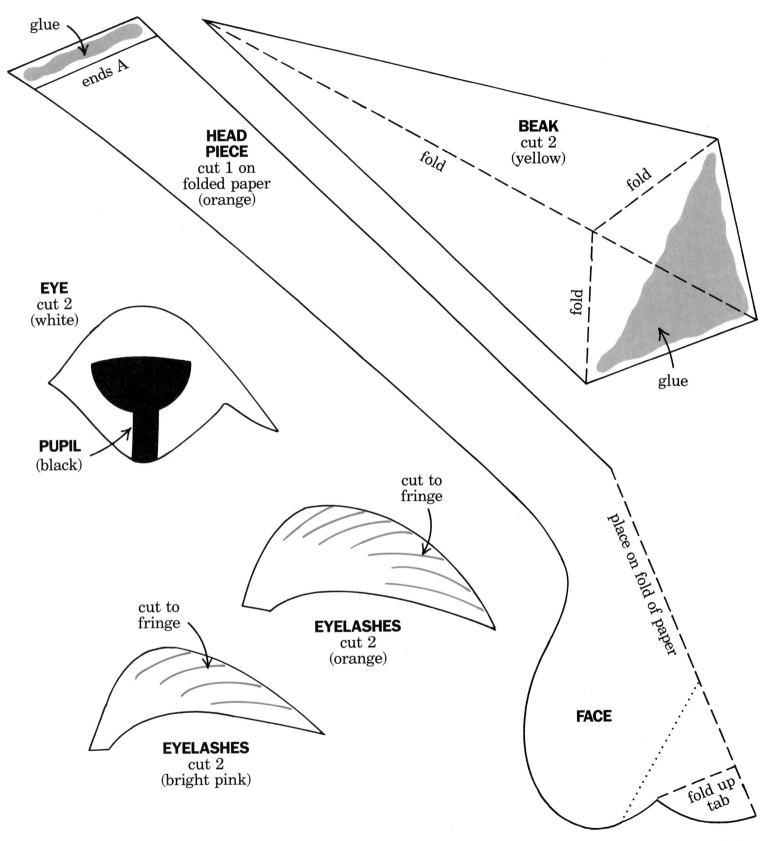

glue

ends A

HEAD PIECE
cut 1 on
folded paper
(orange)

BEAK
cut 2
(yellow)

fold

fold

fold

glue

EYE
cut 2
(white)

PUPIL
(black)

cut to
fringe

cut to
fringe

EYELASHES
cut 2
(orange)

EYELASHES
cut 2
(bright pink)

place on fold of paper

FACE

fold up
tab

131

HIDE & PEEK
CLOWN

Hidden in a plastic cup, this playful puppet makes his appearance when you push up on a stick. Then twist and turn the stick to make him come alive.

TOOLBOX

- 24-ounce plastic drinking cup
- 3-inch plastic foam egg
- 18-inch-long dowel rod, ¼ inch in diameter
- Extra-tacky glue
- Tracing paper
- ¼ yard of knit fabric for shirt
- 9-inch square of white knit fabric to cover egg (you can use an old T-shirt that you've outgrown)
- Scraps of white, red, pink, and green felt for hands and face
- Rubber band
- Four pom-poms for buttons and nose
- Rickrack
- Package of strawberry blond curly hair
- ½ yard of ¼-inch-wide ribbon for bow around neck
- Felt-tip pen
- Manicure scissors
- Stickers

1 Turn the drinking cup upside down. Center one end of the dowel over the center of the cup bottom. Use the felt-tip pen to draw a circle around the dowel end. Cut out the marked circle using the manicure scissors. Continue to trim around the circle until the dowel slips easily through the hole.

2 Push about ½ inch of the dowel into the wide end of the egg. Remove the egg. Squeeze glue around the dowel end and push it back into the egg. Set this piece aside.

TURN THE PAGE ▶

3 Use tracing paper to trace the patterns on pages 136 and 137. Cut out the patterns. Cut two shirt pieces from the knit fabric, being sure to place the fold line of the pattern on the fold of the fabric. Cut the head covering from the white knit fabric. Cut two hands from white felt. Cut the mouth, cheeks, eyes, and eyelids from felt in the colors marked on the pattern pieces.

4 To assemble the shirt, squeeze glue along the edges of the *right side* of one shirt piece. (The pattern shows you the edges where the glue should be placed.) With right sides facing, glue the two shirt pieces together. Set the shirt aside to let the glue dry.

5 Turn the shirt right side out. Fold under the sleeve edges as marked on the pattern. Dab glue on both sides of the hand pieces and glue a hand inside each sleeve.

134

6 Slip a scrap piece of paper behind the front of the shirt and glue three pom-poms down the front. When dry, remove the paper.

8 Squeeze glue over the rubber band. Slip the dowel into the neck of the shirt. Glue the neck to the rubber band. Let the glue dry.

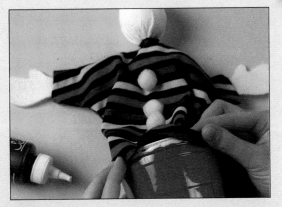

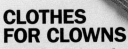

7 Center the white knit circle over the egg and stretch the fabric tightly around the egg. Pleat and fold the excess fabric toward the back of the head. This excess fabric will be covered with the clown's hair. Wrap a rubber band around the bundle of fabric at the bottom of the egg and over the dowel.

9 Squeeze a band of glue around the outside rim of the cup. Fasten the bottom of the shirt to the rim.

10 Squeeze a band of glue around the bottom edges of the shirt. Glue the rickrack to the bottom of the shirt. Begin and end at the back of the puppet.

TURN THE PAGE ▶

CLOTHES FOR CLOWNS

Use brightly colored prints, stripes, or plaids to dress up your clown. Knits work best because they drape nicely, they stretch to fit around the cup, and their edges will not fray.

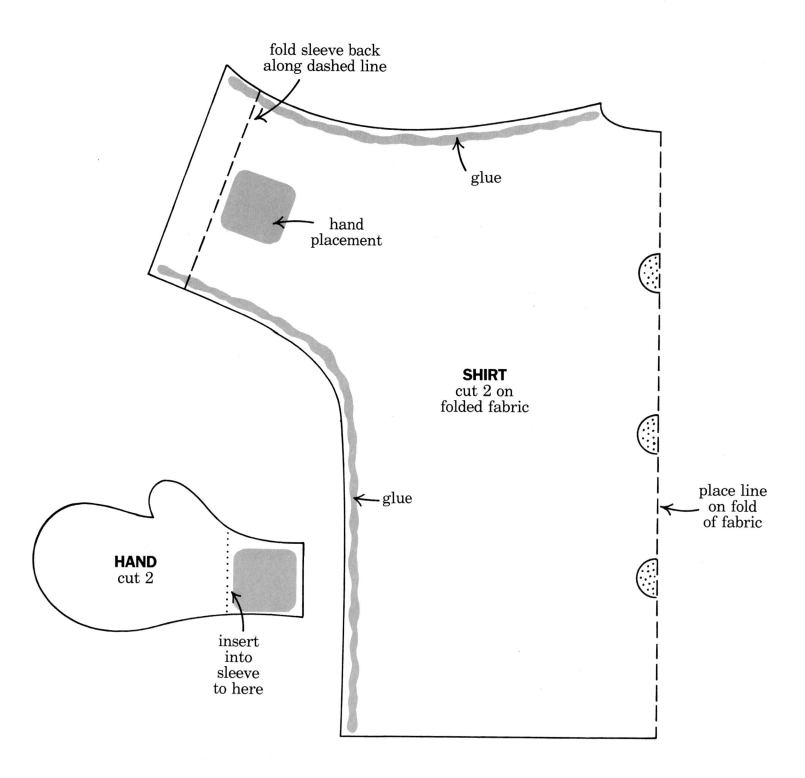

fold sleeve back
along dashed line

glue

hand
placement

glue

SHIRT
cut 2 on
folded fabric

place line
on fold
of fabric

HAND
cut 2

insert
into
sleeve
to here

136

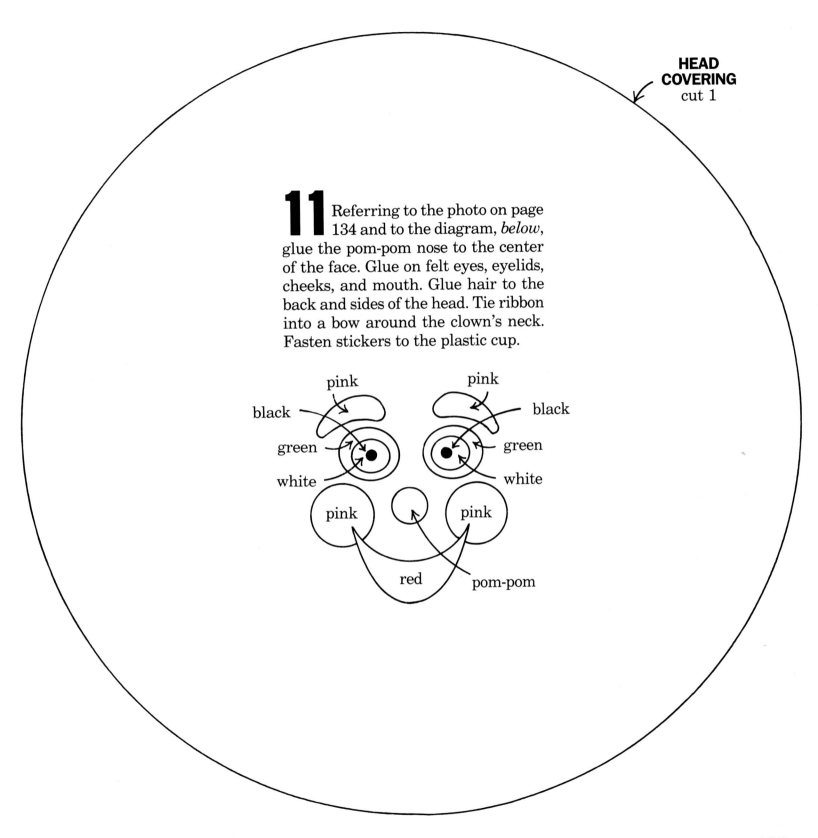

11 Referring to the photo on page 134 and to the diagram, *below*, glue the pom-pom nose to the center of the face. Glue on felt eyes, eyelids, cheeks, and mouth. Glue hair to the back and sides of the head. Tie ribbon into a bow around the clown's neck. Fasten stickers to the plastic cup.

pink

pink

black

black

green

green

white

white

pink

pink

red

pom-pom

Finger Family

We may look fancy but we're simple folks—just party favors, felt, colored papers, and key tags.

I just loved having my photos taken for the how-to steps at right. Our whole family is so stylish.

These bug-eyes are the greatest! They're decorated key tags that you can buy at hardware stores.

TOOLBOX

- ▶ Party blowouts with ½-inch-diameter tubes that will fit over your fingers
- ▶ Key tags for eyes
- ▶ Black, white, and red paper scraps
- ▶ Scraps of pink felt and other colors
- ▶ Tacky glue
- ▶ Two beads
- ▶ Paper punch
- ▶ Black fine felt-tip pen
- ▶ Tracing paper

138

1 For the puppet with the earrings, trace and cut out the arms, hand, shirt, and collar patterns on page 142 from tracing paper. Cut two pink felt hands and one each of the arm, shirt, and collar from felt colors of your choice.

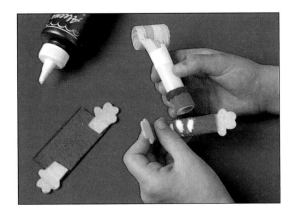

2 Glue the felt shirt around the bottom edge of the blowout tube. Glue the collar along the top edge of the felt shirt.

Glue a hand to each end of the arm piece using the tinted area on the pattern as a guide. Squeeze glue along the top edge of the arm piece. Fold the arm piece in half, using the dashed lines on the pattern as a guide. Glue the top and bottom edges of the arms together. Glue the center of the arm piece to the back of the tube over the shirt.

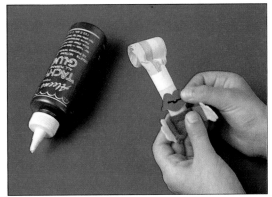

3 Trace and cut out the lips pattern from tracing paper. Draw around the lips pattern on red paper. Cut out the lips. Draw the mouth line on the lips with the felt-tip pen. Glue the lips to the blowout tube.

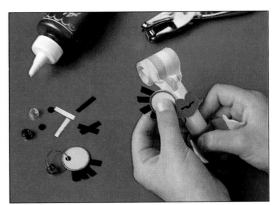

4 For the eyes and earrings, slide beads onto the wires of two key tags. For the eyebrows, cut thin strips of black paper and glue them to the backs of the key tags. Glue the eyes to the blowout tube, placing the earrings at the tube's sides. For the pupils, punch out two black paper dots and glue them to the key tags.

Turn the page and you'll see more finger puppet ideas.

Digital Aliens

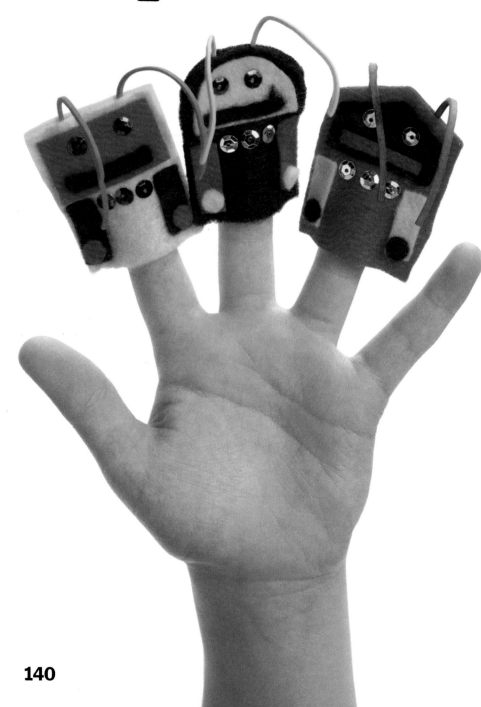

DIGITAL ALIENS Made from scraps of felt and sequin trims, these friendly folks from outer space are easy to put together with glue. See page 142 *(middle column)* for the patterns. Referring to the photo *at left,* glue the head, arms, and mouth pieces onto one of the body pieces. Use a paper punch to punch out felt dots for the hands. For the antennae, cut a rubber band into two equal lengths. Glue the rubber band pieces to the back of the body (about ¼ inch from the top). Glue two matching body pieces together, leaving the bottom edge unglued. Glue on sequins to decorate the puppets as you like. Let the glue dry.

WESTERN WIGGLERS A 3-inch-long spring that fits over your finger is the beginning of a puppet in this trio. For the body clothing, cut a felt rectangle that fits around the spring with a ¼-inch overlap. Glue the rectangle to the spring. For one arm, glue two narrow strips of felt together to make a tube. Thread a small bead on one end of the tube. Glue the other end to the side of the felt-covered spring. Make a second arm following the same instructions. Glue other felt details to the body as you wish, using the photo *at right* as a guide. Glue a large bead to the top of the spring for the head. Use a felt-tip pen to draw eyes and a mouth. Glue yarn or fur to the head for hair.

Western Wigglers

FINGERTIP CLOWNS Cut off the fingers of a rubber glove about 2½ inches from the tips. Turn the fingers inside out. Use the patterns on page 142 *(right column)* to cut out a felt mouth, collar, bow tie, shirt, and paper hat. Use a tiny red pom-pom for a nose. Glue on wiggle eyes. Use pompoms of other colors for buttons or trim on the collar or shirt. Use cotton balls for hair. Glue on the hat, decorating it with punched paper dots.

Fingertip CLOWNS

Patterns for Finger Family

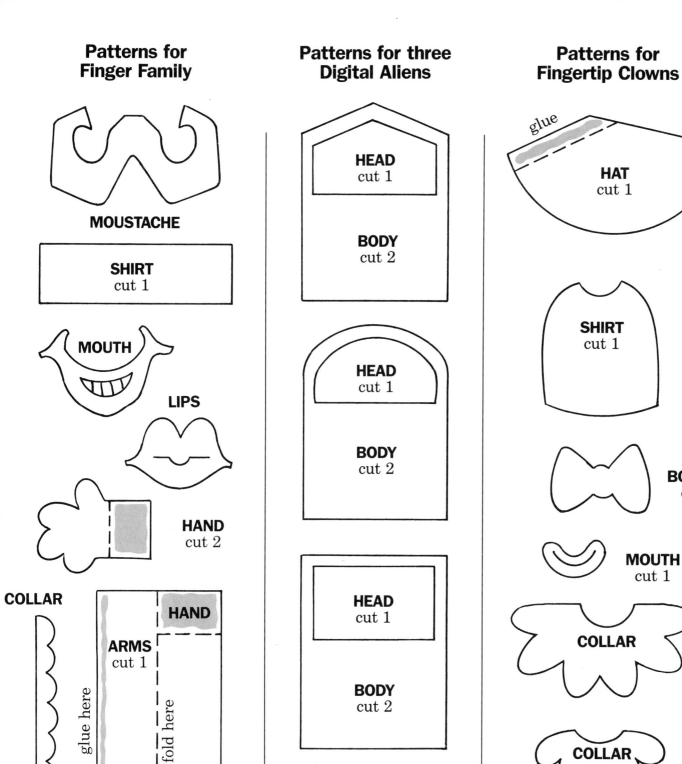

MOUSTACHE

SHIRT
cut 1

MOUTH

LIPS

HAND
cut 2

COLLAR

glue here

ARMS
cut 1

HAND

fold here

HAND

Patterns for three Digital Aliens

HEAD
cut 1

BODY
cut 2

HEAD
cut 1

BODY
cut 2

HEAD
cut 1

BODY
cut 2

ARM
cut 2

MOUTH
cut 1

Patterns for Fingertip Clowns

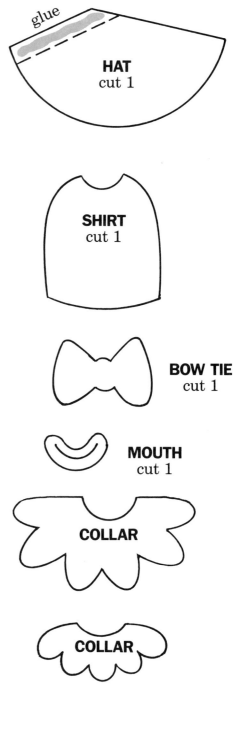

glue

HAT
cut 1

SHIRT
cut 1

BOW TIE
cut 1

MOUTH
cut 1

COLLAR

COLLAR

DAZZLING DOLLS

Bobby and the Sockettes

Doo Wah
Doo Wah

Sh-Boom
Sh-Boom

Who would have guessed that you can turn ordinary socks into a group of rock stars! We show you how to make the yellow singer. You can use these same directions to make the other two.

TOOLBOX

- ▶ Brightly colored crew socks
- ▶ Rice
- ▶ Fiberfill
- ▶ String
- ▶ Sewing needle
- ▶ Yellow, red, and purple sewing threads
- ▶ Buttons for eyes
- ▶ Pom-poms
- ▶ Tacky glue
- ▶ Scraps of red and white felt, ribbon, and rickrack
- ▶ White cardboard for feet
- ▶ Felt-tip pens

1 For the body, pour 1 cup of rice into the toe of one sock. Flatten the toe to shape a 3-inch-diameter circle. Stuff the remaining foot and heel with fiberfill. Do not stuff the sock above the ribbing.

2 Tightly wrap the string at the top of the fiberfill and tie a knot.

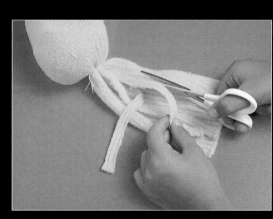

3 For the hair, cut the ribbed part of the sock into ½-inch-wide strands. Cut to within ½ inch of the tied string. Tie overhand knots at the ends of each strand.

TURN THE PAGE ▶

TIPS ABOUT SOCKS

It's best to use crew socks, not tube socks, to make these dolls. Crew socks are the kind that have ribbing only above the ankle. The foot and heel do not have ribbing. We used bright, solid colors to make our rock stars, but striped, plaid, and other patterned socks could make hilarious and clever dolls, too.

FOR BOBBY, THE GUITARIST

Stuff the sock according to Step 1 of the instructions. Knot the string around the sock at the top of the fiberfill. Cut off the ribbed part of the sock. Shape the eyes and mouth. For hair, glue a 1½x6-inch strip of fake fur across the top of the head. For the hat, cut off the ribbed portion of another colored sock. Gather and sew the cut edge together. Glue a pom-pom to the top of the gathers. Use the patterns on page 149 to make a cardboard guitar and feet.

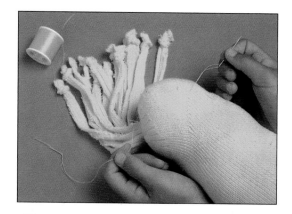

4 To mark the position for the mouth, thread the needle with a double strand of yellow thread. Insert the needle in the top of the head, close to the string, and bring the needle out at the end of one of the heel seams. Take the needle back into the same heel seam and bring the needle out at the top of the head. Pull both ends of the thread to pull in a dimple at the heel seam. Knot the thread and cut.

Repeat this step to make a dimple using the heel seam on the other side.

For the mouth, thread the needle with a double strand of red thread. Insert the needle through one dimple stitch on one side of the head and bring it out through the dimple stitch on the other side of the head. Take the thread across the front of the face and into the first dimple stitch and out through the other dimple stitch. Do not cut the thread.

From red felt, cut out the lips using the pattern on page 148. Center the lips over the red stitch and sew them in place. Knot and clip the thread.

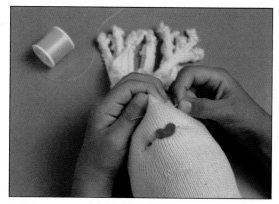

5 For the eye indents, thread the needle with a double strand of yellow thread. Pinch together the sides of the sock above the mouth. Insert the needle through the pinched portion and pull tightly on the thread. Take the needle back through the pinched portion and tie the thread ends into a knot. Clip the thread.

6 About 1 inch down from the eye indents, make a long stitch to shape the nose. Slightly tug on the thread to form the tip of the nose. Knot the thread. Sew on buttons for eyes where the indents were made in Step 5. Use thread to sew long eyelashes or glue on felt eyelashes.

7 For the sweater, trace the sleeve and hand patterns on page 148. Refer to the sock photo at *right* to cut out the sleeves and body for the sweater from one sock.

Hand-sew the sleeve side seams, leaving the wrist area open. Turn the sleeves right side out. Cut out two felt hands. Insert one hand into each of the wrist openings and hand-sew the openings closed. Sew or glue rick-rack to the ends of the sleeves.

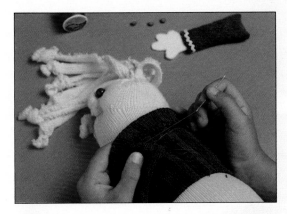

8 Slip the sweater body piece over the doll. Turn *under* the cut edge at the waist. Turn *over* the top edge at the neck. Sew the sleeves to the sides of the sweater. Trim the sweater with three pom-pom buttons.

9 Trace the buckled shoe pattern on page 148. Cut out the pattern from cardboard. Color the shoes with the felt pens. Glue the shoes to the doll. Prop the doll to let the glue dry.

Twist the ribbon to shape a bow and sew it to the top of the head.

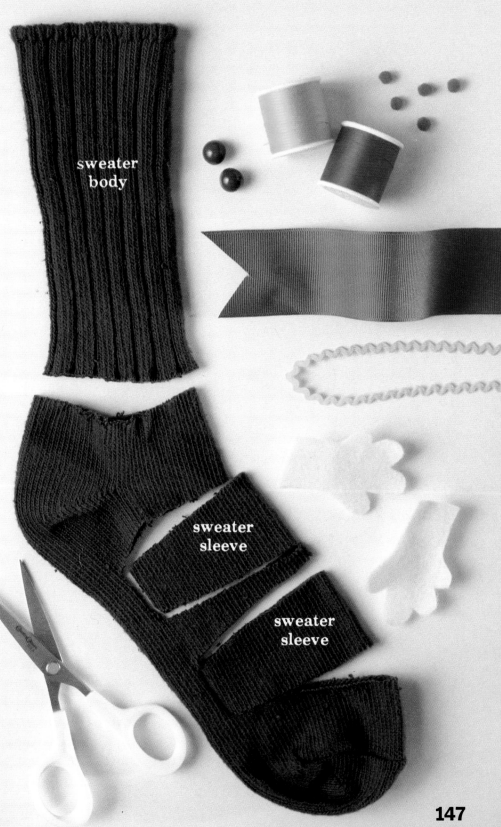

sweater body

sweater sleeve

sweater sleeve

Patterns for Sock Dolls

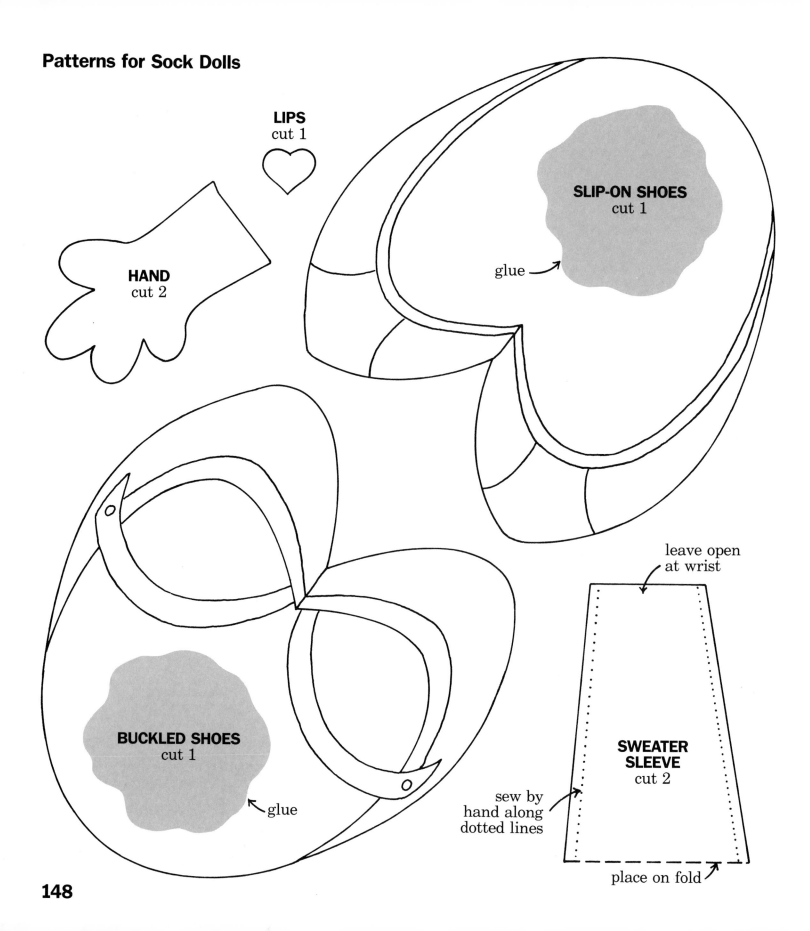

LIPS
cut 1

HAND
cut 2

SLIP-ON SHOES
cut 1

glue

BUCKLED SHOES
cut 1

glue

leave open
at wrist

**SWEATER
SLEEVE**
cut 2

sew by
hand along
dotted lines

place on fold

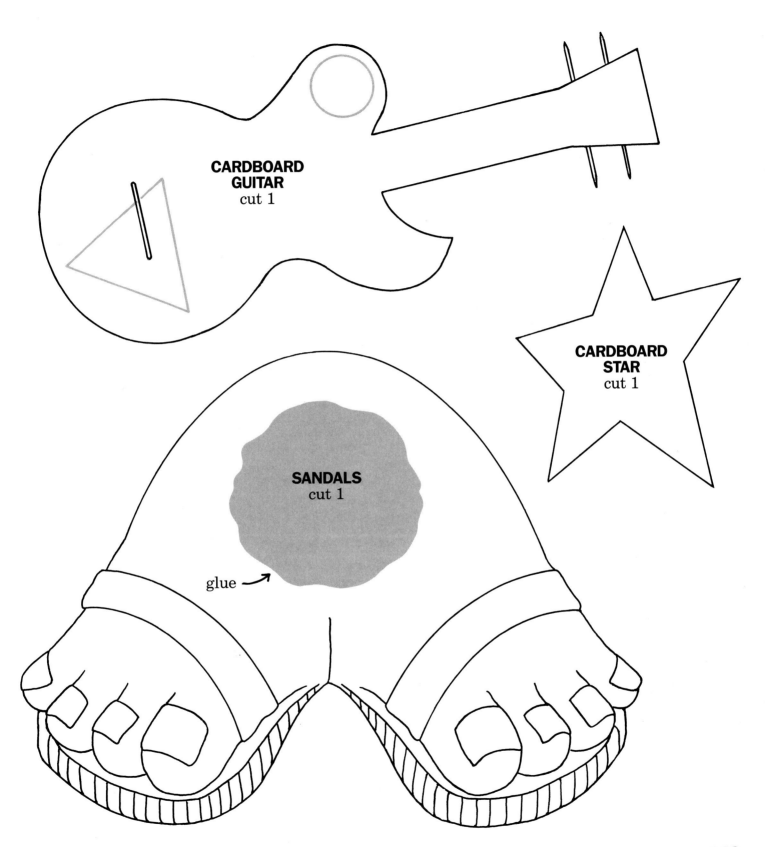

CARDBOARD GUITAR
cut 1

CARDBOARD STAR
cut 1

SANDALS
cut 1

glue

Paper Pals

These two friends have clothes for every season and every occasion. Their outfits are made from a fabric interfacing that's easy to color. No-sew self-grip fastening tabs are stuck to the dolls and their clothing for easy dressing.

TOOLBOX

- ▶ ⅔ yard of heavy white interfacing
- ▶ Crayons
- ▶ Felt-tip black markers (1 wide-tip and 1 fine-tip)
- ▶ Tracing paper
- ▶ Scissors
- ▶ Poster board
- ▶ No. 2 pencil
- ▶ Straight pin
- ▶ No-sew self-grip fastening tabs

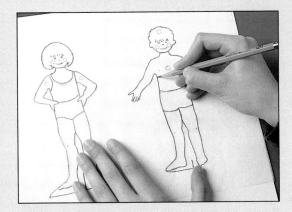

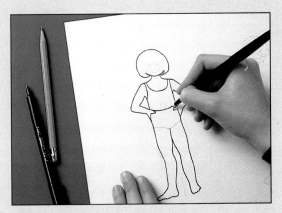

1 Trace the doll and stand patterns on page 153 onto tracing paper. With the No. 2 pencil, trace over the drawn lines on the *back* side of the tracing. Turn the tracing over. With the front side up, place it on top of the poster board. Draw over the traced lines to transfer the tracing to the poster board.

2 Outline the poster board dolls with the wide felt-tip marker. Use the fine-tip marker to outline the dashed cheek lines and the underwear trim. Stick the fastening tabs (flatter circles) to the dolls following the pattern placements.

3 Color the dolls. Cut out the dolls and the doll stands.

4 For the clothing, cut a piece of interfacing the size of one of the outfits on pages 154–157. Lay the interfacing over the outfit and trace the pattern.

TURN THE PAGE ▶

TIPS FOR CLOTHING You can use plain white paper to make the clothing for the dolls. If you cannot see through the paper to draw the patterns, use tracing paper and follow Step 1 of the instructions for tracing the dolls on page 151. Then trace the patterns onto the plain white paper.

If you want, add paper tabs at the shoulders of the outfits and at the tops of the hats as another way to fasten the clothing to the dolls. Add the tabs before you cut out the outfits.

Once you have made our designs, try drawing and coloring clothes for the dolls that match some of yours. Lay the dolls on the paper and lightly draw around the body shape. Then design and draw the clothing using the body drawing as a guide.

5 Outline the outfit with the wide-tip marker and the details with the fine-tip marker. Color the clothing using the pattern as a guide, or using colors of your choice. Cut out the outfit.

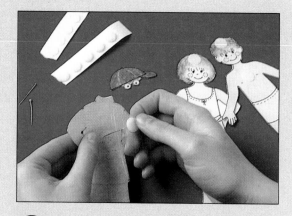

6 Position the outfit on the doll. Gently push the straight pin through the clothing into the fastening tab on the doll. Keeping the straight pin in the outfit, remove the clothing from the doll. Use the pin as a placement guide to fasten the matching fastening tab to the back side of the outfit.

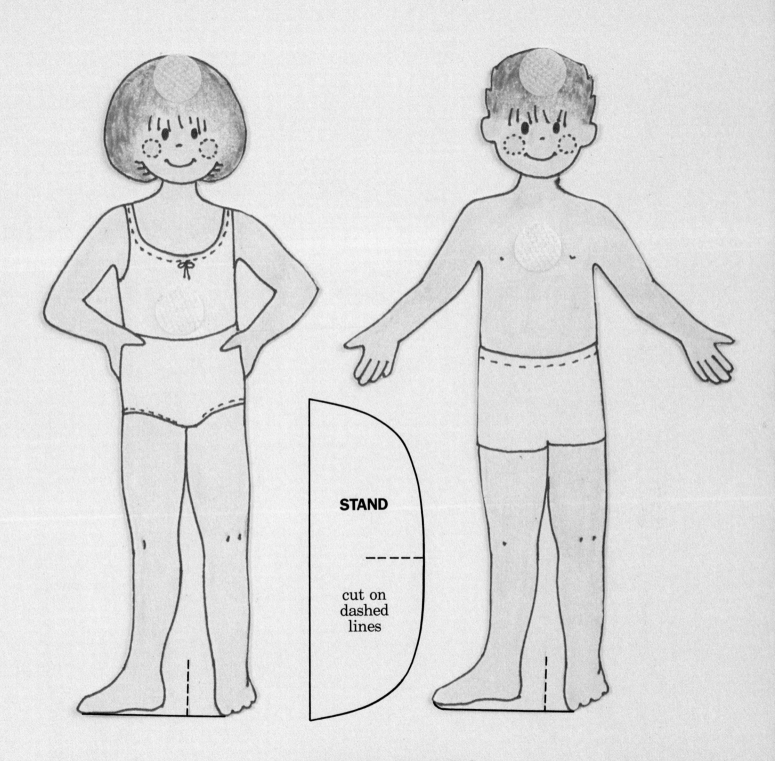

STAND

cut on
dashed
lines

Patterns for Paper Pals

153

Patterns for boy's clothing

155

Patterns for girl's clothing

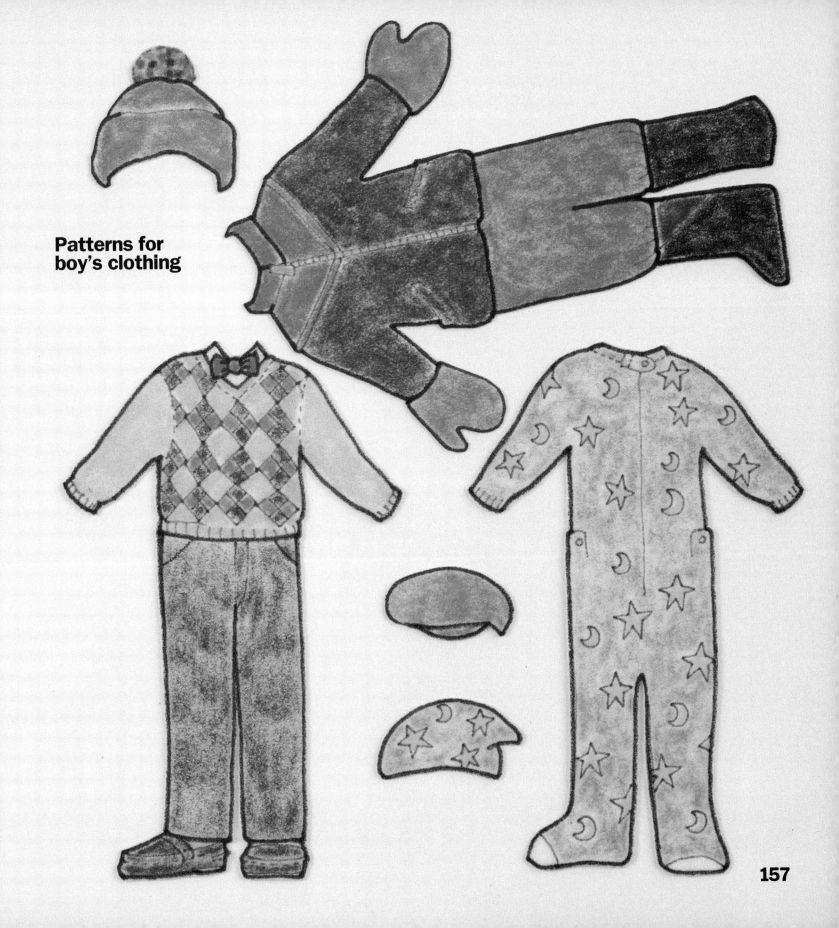

Patterns for boy's clothing

157

TEENY TEENS

Wrap and wind embroidery floss around toothpicks to make every kind of fashionable doll imaginable. Then use them to trim barrettes, earrings, pins, or to create a family of dollhouse dolls.

TOOLBOX

- ▶ Square-center round toothpicks
- ▶ Ruler
- ▶ Scissors
- ▶ Pencil
- ▶ Crafts glue
- ▶ Assorted colors of embroidery floss for hair, skin, and clothing

1 Cut off ⅝ inch from both ends of one toothpick for the body.
Cut off ⅝ inch from one end of two toothpicks for the legs.
Cut off 1½ inches from one end of two toothpicks for the arms.

2 On the body, use the pencil to mark ⅝ inch in from one end. Glue the legs to the sides of the body with the uncut tips at the mark.

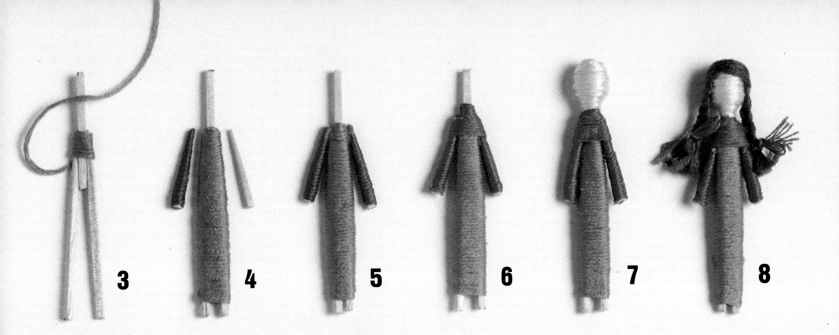

3 **4** **5** **6** **7** **8**

3 Begin wrapping the floss for the dress at the mark. Dab glue on the ends of the floss to secure them to the back of the doll. Wrap the floss down the legs to the desired length.

4 Using another color of floss, wrap each arm.

5 Glue the arms to the body at the mark.

6 Wrap the floss slightly above and below the mark to shape the neck and shoulders.

7 To shape the head, wrap the skin-color floss around the body above the mark.

8 Add a favorite hairstyle, creating ponytails, braids, or lots of curls.

TUMBLING TERRY

These tumbling marble-head dolls bring wonderment and smiles to all those who see them perform.

HOW TO MAKE YOUR DOLL TUMBLE
Place the doll at the top of a slanted board and it immediately will begin to somersault. If the doll is stubborn, increase the slope of the board. If the board's surface is too slick, the doll may not tumble as well. Cover it with some fabric to create friction.

TOOLBOX

- ▶ 1-inch-diameter marble
- ▶ Tracing paper
- ▶ Heavyweight pink construction or Canson paper
- ▶ Black ballpoint pen
- ▶ Toothpick
- ▶ Waxed paper
- ▶ Thin terry washcloth
- ▶ Tacky glue
- ▶ ¼-inch-wide ribbon

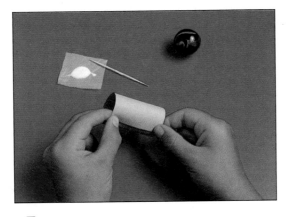

1 Trace the small head, hand, and foot patterns on page 163 onto tracing paper. Cut out the patterns. Cut the patterns from the pink paper. Use the pen to draw facial features on the head using the pattern as a guide. Glue the edges of the head piece together to make a tube.

3 Trace and cut out two small body patterns on page 163 from the washcloth. Following the glue line on the pattern, squeeze glue around the outside edges of one body piece. Place the hands and feet in position over the glue. Glue the two body pieces together. Let the glue dry.

2 Trace the small crown pattern on page 162 onto tracing paper. Cut out the pattern. Cut two crowns from the washcloth. Glue one crown to one end of the head. Insert the marble inside the head and glue the second crown to the other end of the head. Set the head aside to dry.

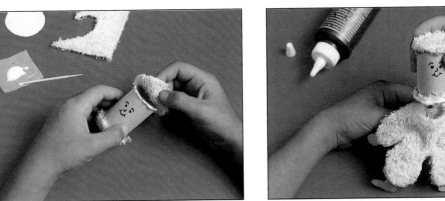

4 Run a band of glue around the neck of the head. Slip the head into the body and fasten the neck of the body to the head. Tie a ribbon into a bow around the neck. Spot-glue the ribbon to hold it in place.

TUMBLING CLOWN Use the *large* patterns, *below* and on page 163, to make a large clown doll that also does somersaults. Follow the steps on page 161 but put a golf ball inside the head, instead of a marble, to make him tumble.

SMALL CROWN cut 2

LARGE CROWN cut 2

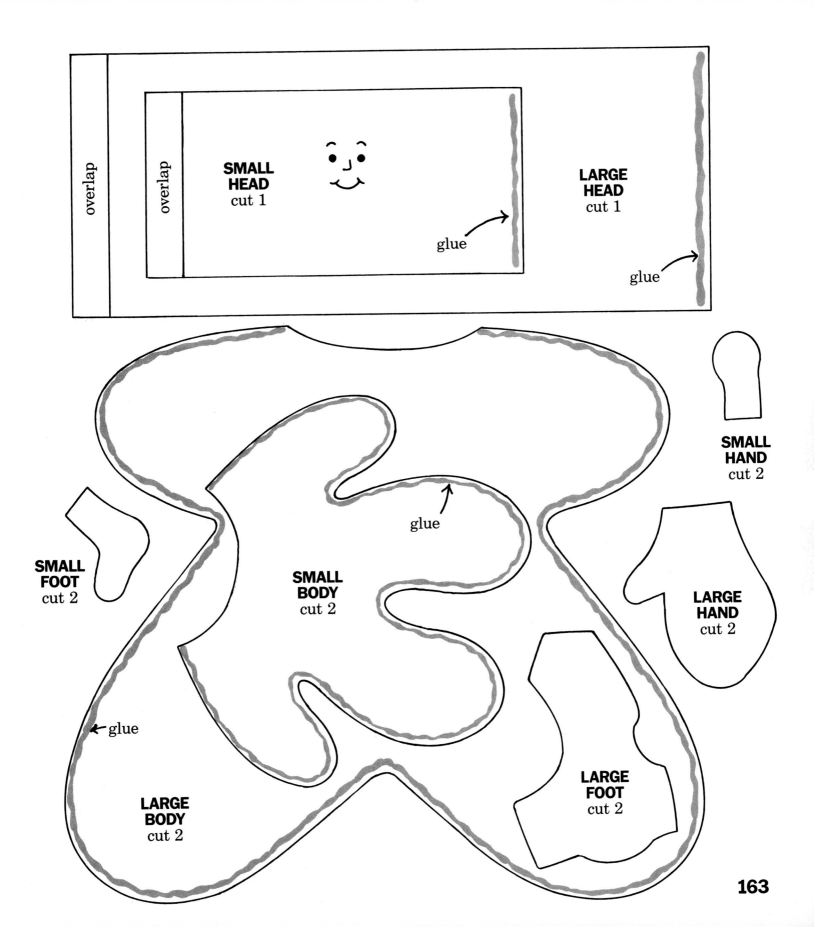

overlap

overlap

SMALL HEAD
cut 1

glue

LARGE HEAD
cut 1

glue

SMALL HAND
cut 2

SMALL FOOT
cut 2

SMALL BODY
cut 2

glue

LARGE HAND
cut 2

glue

LARGE FOOT
cut 2

LARGE BODY
cut 2

BOUNCY
BEAD
B·U·D·D·I·E·S

Gather some wooden beads and rubber bands to make a bouncy bead doll that is sure to make you smile.

TOOLBOX

▶ Three large wooden beads for head and body
▶ Five smaller wooden beads for hands, feet, and top of hat
▶ One wooden disc or wheel for hat
▶ Acrylic paints
▶ Toothpicks
▶ Fine paintbrush
▶ ¼-inch flat paintbrush
▶ Tacky glue
▶ Three rubber bands

1 Paint all the beads with acrylic paints using the dolls *above* as a guide or using colors of your choice. Place a toothpick through the holes of the beads to make them easy to hold as you paint. Let the paint dry. Use the fine paintbrush to decorate two of the large beads. Do not paint the face on a bead at this time.

2 Glue the three large beads together. Notice the locations of the holes in the beads as you glue them together. To make it easy to glue them, butt them together on a flat surface. Let the glue dry completely before you continue to the next step.

3 Refer to the diagram at *right* to add the arms and legs to the body beads. First, cut the rubber bands into long strands. Tie an overhand knot in one end of *two* rubber bands. Thread a small bead onto each of the knotted bands. Push one band through the hole in each of the two body beads. Slip another small bead on the end of each band. Tie an overhand knot at the end of each band.

4 For the head, thread a rubber band through the hat bead, the disc, the head bead, back through the disc, and hat bead. Knot the ends of the rubber band together. Paint the face using the fine brush.

THREADING THE BEADS If you have difficulty pushing the rubber bands through the beads, use a straight pin to guide them through the holes. If you have a large-eye needle, you can thread it with the rubber band, insert the needle through the bead, and pull the band through.

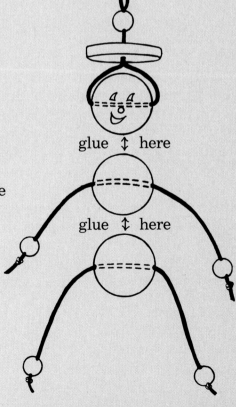

glue ↕ here

glue ↕ here

165

READY, SET, CRAFT

Browse through this book and select a project that you want to make. On the opposite page there are some ideas for special occasions—Easter, Christmas, birthdays—that may help you choose a project for a specific event. But before you begin any project, read through the following tips. They'll help you get started.

Read over the items in the Toolbox for the project you selected. This list of materials tells you everything you need to collect in order to make the project that is shown in the photograph.

Gather together all the materials listed in the Toolbox before you begin. You probably have some of these items in your home. Crafts glue, waxed paper, tracing paper, a pencil, scissors, and a ruler are among some of the general supplies. Check with your parents. They'll have lots of these things on hand. You may have to buy specific items such as tissue papers, felt, cork, paints, or beads, at an art, crafts, or variety store.

Protect your work area with newspaper, waxed paper, paper towels, or aluminum foil. From time to time, you may find it necessary to put down another layer of cover-up material to protect your project from spilled glue or paints. Clean up your work area when your project is complete.

Read the how-to steps and examine the photos that go with the steps. They explain the order for making the project. Not all the steps have how-to photos. We chose photos we thought would make certain steps clearer.

Some of the projects require patterns. These patterns always are provided and are full-size. Trace the patterns from the book using tracing paper. Then cut out the tracing paper patterns and draw around them onto the crafting material. When a pattern has a dashed line with the phrase "cut on folded paper," that means after you cut out the tissue pattern, you draw around the pattern on the *folded* crafting material. When you cut out the crafting material, *do not* cut along the fold line. When you unfold the material, you will have a complete piece.

From time to time throughout this book, we found that some of the crafting techniques or materials could be used to make different projects. For example, we show you on pages 62 and 63 how to make a picture frame out of puzzle pieces. By following these same instructions, you can make a picture frame using map paper, music paper, or gift wrap. And, you can turn to pages 64 and 65 to find other creative ideas for using puzzle pieces.

We did not indicate a skill or age level for the projects in this book. Let your imagination, your interests, and your skills determine the ones that you want to make. As you continue to craft and have success, you will gain the confidence to try those projects that appear to be more difficult.

WHAT DO YOU WANT TO MAKE?

ACKNOWLEDGMENTS

We express our gratitude and appreciation to the many people who helped produce this book. Our heartfelt thanks go to all the designers who helped create the projects for this book, to the young people who modeled and patiently helped us with the photo project steps, and to the photographers for their creative talents.

DESIGNERS

Finley D. Harper Black—74–75; 76–77

Carol Field Dahlstrom—88–89

Phyllis Dunstan—47; 48–49; 63; 64–65; 82, mask; 90–91; 92–93; 124–125; 138–139; 141, western finger puppets; 144–145

Stacey Edwards—100

Martha Ehrlich—18–19; 20, gift wrap; 40; 140–141, alien and clown finger puppets; 164–165

Kathy Engel—150–151

Chris Hamner—20, cards and bookmarks; 22–25; 26-27; 32–34

Lezlie Kohrs and Sara Mahr for DMC—158–159

Sara Mahr and Lezlie Kohrs for DMC—158–159

Warren Neubauer—104–105; 106–107

Deborah Pappenheimer—8–9; 12–13; 14–15; 36–37; 44–45; 85; 86–87; 121; 162

Dara Lea Saunders and Cara Veeder—94–95; 96–97

Karen Taylor—96–97

Suzie Treinen—54–55; 58–59; 60–61; 68; 70–71; 80; 82–83, bowls and piñata; 108; 111

Tom Treinen—50–51

Cara Veeder and Dara Lea Saunders—94–95; 96–97

Judith Veeder—10–11

MODELS

Walter Bruty
Roberta Craddock
Erik Granseth
Aubrey Howard
Devon Howard
Gabe Johnson
Jackie Jones
Mary Meagan Manroe
Schuyler Paul
Lexie Sipes
Tori Sipes
Suzie Treinen
Cara Veeder
Andrew Vermie
Christina Wilson-Carraro
Justin Woodard

PHOTOGRAPHERS

Scott Little—158
Perry Struse—cover and all remaining photos

If you would like to order any additional copies of our books, call 1-800-678-2803 or check with your local bookstore.